FEARLESS REMODELING!

A PLANNING GUIDE FOR THE HOMEOWNER

SUSAN DIAMOND LUXENBERG

1999 Susan Diamond Luxenberg

Book Design by Kathryn Seely
Illustrations by K^2 Designs

First Edition
10 9 8 7 6 5 4 3 2 1
Printed in Canada

Library of Congress Catalog Card No: 99-095451

ISBN 0-9673383-0-1

Homesmart Consulting Inc.
PO Box 18306
Rochester, New York 14618-8306
www.homesmart.org

To my daughters,

Stephanie & Amy,

with much love

ACKNOWLEDGMENTS

In my 20 years in the building business, there have been many who have contributed to my knowledge and experience, and consequently to this book. While impossible to list everyone within these constraints, I would like to thank those who have been helpful along the way. I'd also like to thank all the homeowners whose questions and concerns were the impetus to this book.

A special thank you to Ben Kendig, who gave me a break and taught me a business that changed my life forever. Special thanks also to Barb Farron for knowing I had a book to write and starting me down that road.

To those who worked on this book: My thanks to Vicki Brown for her editorial expertise and Kathryn Seely for her creative and spirited design. Thank you to Stephen Smock for his wonderful illustrations, to Max Gershenoff and CopyWrite Communications for their inspired direction, and to Chris Young at Hignell Book Printing for his patience and commitment to produce my vision. A heartfelt thank you to Amy Horowitz for her skillful transatlantic editing and to Stephanie Luxenberg, whose insights regarding content added immeasurably to this book.

To the family and friends who listened endlessly as I made my way through the writing process - thank you for your advice, confidence, and patience.

And last, but certainly not least, a loving thank you to my parents without whose encouragement and support this never would have happened.

TABLE OF CONTENTS

HOW TO GET THE RESULTS YOU WANT 11

STEP 1 DEFINE YOUR PROJECT 19

Get Organized 19
Start a Wishlist 22
    Worksheet: Wishlist 25
Define Your Space Requirements 27
Preliminary Design Concepts 28
    Worksheet: Sketch of Existing Layout 31
            Sketch of New Plan 33
Tips: Planning & Design 35

STEP 2 DETERMINE REALISTIC COSTS 39

Investigate Housing Values 40
Financing Options 41
    Worksheet: Financial 45
The Preliminary Budget 47
    Worksheet: Preliminary Costs .49
Establish Priorities 51
    Worksheet: Project Priorities .53
Tips: Smart Budgeting 57

STEP 3 PREPARE A DESCRIPTION OF YOUR PLAN 61

Permits & Regulations 61
    Worksheet: Project Drawing 63
Professional Help 65
    Worksheet: Designer's References 69
The Importance of Specifications 71
    Worksheet: Specifications 79
The Bid Sheet 81
    Worksheet: Bid Sheet 85
Checklist for Preparing Plans and Specs 87

◢STEP 4 FIND REPUTABLE CONTRACTORS TO BID 91

The Bidding Process 91
Interview Contractors 92
    Worksheet: Contractor Interview 97
Client and Credit References 99
    Worksheet: Contractor's References 101
Checklist for the Bidding Process 103

◢STEP 5 EVALUATE & COMPARE THE BIDS 107

Why Bids Vary 107
How to Review a Bid 108
    Worksheet: Individual Bid Review 109
Comparing Bids 115
    Worksheet: Bid Comparison 117
Options for Reducing Costs 119
Checklist for Selecting a Contractor .121

◢STEP 6 PROTECT YOURSELF WITH A SOLID CONTRACT 125

Types of agreements 126
Contract Basics 127
Contract Price and Change Orders 128
Lien Waivers 130
Sample Contract 130
General Provisions 134
    Worksheet: Contract Information 139

◢STEP 7 OVERSEE THE WORK IN PROGRESS 145

The Pre-Construction Meeting 145
The 6 Principles of Project Management 146
Stages of Construction 149
Your Final Inspection 155
Checklist for Project Completion 157
    Worksheet: Punchlist 159

APPENDICES 163

Appendix A: Construction Standards 165
Appendix B: Contract, Lien Waiver, & Change Order Form 175
Appendix C: Worksheets 187

How to Get the Results You Want

Throughout my career, I have worked with a variety of clients on hundreds of different projects large and small, yet the concerns and questions are always the same:

Where do I start?
Will I need an architect?
What makes sense for my budget?
How do I select a reputable contractor?
How do I explain what I want?
How do I know I'm not getting taken?
How can I keep the costs down?
How can I evaluate the quality of the work done?

Most people are overwhelmed before they even begin! When faced with managing a remodeling or building project, homeowners worry about their lack of expertise and technical knowledge, fear there's too much they don't understand, and become anxious about losing control over their money and homes because they're dependent on others to execute their plans. As if this were not enough, they also carry around myths about the construction industry that set up feelings of mistrust from the start.

We've all heard stories from family, friends or neighbors who have completed home building projects. Some of them are extremely happy with the results. They talk excitedly about the wonderful contractor they used, how smoothly the job went, how happy they were with the finished product. Given the opportunity, they'd do it again. They had *fun*. Others, however, have very different stories to tell. Their projects were nightmares. Their contractors failed to show up on time, their homes were left in a mess, the costs far exceeded their budgets. They never want to see another contractor again! What made the experience so different? Was it the specific contractor they used? Or was it just luck?

Successful projects I've managed have all had certain things in common. The homeowners had a clear vision of what they wanted to accomplish and were able to convey their vision to others. These homeowners stayed relaxed and enjoyed the remodeling experience because they were informed, had realistic expectations and anticipated what would be required of them. While there may have been occasional frustrations and compromises (which are normal on any building job), there were no unpleasant surprises. The projects went smoothly because everyone involved had the same information, kept communication lines open, and respected each other's needs.

How, then, do you ensure success? The key is to recognize that *remodeling is a process* that begins long before the first workman arrives at your door. To get what you want requires taking the time to plan before construction begins. Planning is essential to your job running smoothly and minimizing confusion and disappointment. To effectively plan your remodeling project, you'll need to research designs, products and costs, investigate people with whom to work, learn how to communicate your ideas clearly and consistently, develop appropriate contract documents, and understand how to monitor the work. If you've planned your project well, you won't need technical knowledge or construction expertise. Good planning will allow you to relax and enjoy the remodeling experience.

This book is intended to demystify what many believe is a confusing, and often difficult, process. Managing a remodeling project does not have to be difficult. Just follow the seven steps outlined - one step at a time - and you'll gain the knowledge and skill to approach your project with confidence and achieve the results you want.

Your building project can be fun and rewarding. You are about to create living space that you and your family will enjoy for many years to come. My hope is that by using the tools provided in this book, you, too, will become a satisfied homeowner, looking forward to your next remodeling project.

Keep to successful

Communicate; written
, Send updates on the project
weekly by email

HOW TO USE THIS BOOK

Each chapter prepares you for a step in the building/remodeling process.
Read the introductory material in the chapter, then use the chapter worksheets to clarify your thoughts and organize information for your project. There are no "right" or "wrong" ways to fill in the worksheets. They are your project management tools. Whether you decide to handle each step yourself or hire professionals for one or more steps along the way, the worksheets form the foundation of your plan. Follow the steps in order and complete each step before moving on to the next.

Look for this symbol throughout the book for worksheet instructions.

Note: For ease of use, Appendix C provides copies of all worksheets found in the individual chapters. The appendices also contain a guide to quality standards and a complete set of contract documents.

The 7 Steps

1. DEFINE YOUR PROJECT

2. DETERMINE REALISTIC COSTS

3. PREPARE A DESCRIPTION OF YOUR PLAN

4. FIND REPUTABLE CONTRACTORS TO BID

5. EVALUATE AND COMPARE THE BIDS

6. PROTECT YOURSELF WITH A SOLID CONTRACT

7. OVERSEE THE WORK IN PROGRESS

Where Do I Start?

Define Your Project

The first step to creating a successful building or remodeling project is to figure out exactly what it is you want to accomplish. Given the range of products and options for design in today's market, it can be intimidating to try to find exactly the right things that meet your needs and expectations. Investigating different options well before your remodeling begins will give you plenty of time to make decisions without being pressured. Do yourself a favor - research and plan now in order to prevent stress later. The better prepared you are before the work begins, the smoother your job will go and the less it will cost.

Few homeowners end up with the same plan they initially conceived. As you research designs, discuss your project with friends and family, and talk to salespeople about the advantages and disadvantages of different products, you will begin to formulate new ideas and perhaps even find new solutions to old problems.

GET ORGANIZED

Start a project notebook or binder so you can organize and collect design and product information as you develop your ideas. Buy a set of dividers and mark each with the following categories:

- questions & notes
- pictures & photos
- product information
- sketches & plans
- contractor & designer references
- estimates
- invoices & receipts
- schedules
- contract documents

Visit Model Homes

Don't be surprised if you find it hard to visualize what your concept will look like when it's built. Most people have difficulty envisioning the end result. That's one of the reasons why homebuilders go to great lengths to decorate model homes. They know prospective clients need more than a set of blueprints to understand whether a house or room fits their lifestyle. By walking through some model homes, you will get a clearer sense of how different designs suit your personal style.

Picture Your Room Furnished

Homeowners tend to think of interior design as the icing on the cake and don't begin to seriously consider it until construction is nearly complete. Yet how a room is utilized and decorated is definitely affected by window and door placement, built-ins, lighting and outlet locations. It's very disappointing to spend money and time to update your home, only to find out once the construction is nearly finished that the room can't accommodate the furniture you love or you forgot to include enough outlets for your entertainment center components. When you can picture your new room furnished you will, in fact, have formed the basis for your construction plan. At that point, you can start to work backwards from the finished product, selecting those items necessary to achieve the results you want. Using this approach will also make it a lot easier for you to weed through the seemingly endless array of products and designs available today.

Clip Pictures From Magazines

For now, jot down your design ideas and any questions or concerns you might have. Look through decorating and remodeling magazines and cut out pictures of rooms or specific products you like. If you find plans, photos or pictures showing some or all of the elements you want in your own project, you'll be able to use them as guides as you design, get prices, select materials and work with a contractor. As you look through magazines and catalogues, you may find pictures of rooms you like without being able to articulate their appeal. Save them anyway. As you continue researching, these pictures will help you refine your design ideas. Seeing a finished and decorated room in a magazine is one step away from walking through a model home, and can help you make decisions about your own project.

KNOW YOUR PRODUCT OPTIONS

Whether you are planning a large addition or a simpler remodeling job, you'll want to explore the many products available in the marketplace, along with options for design and cost. Go to showrooms and retail building stores to collect product brochures and prices. When you get home, put the information into your notebook for future reference. If you've brought home a pamphlet on a product that you really don't need or like, toss it. Keep only the product information that helps you clarify your project needs.

Researching ideas and organizing the materials and information you acquire will help you make informed, thoughtful decisions and avoid hasty ones that lead to disappointment.

ATTEND HOME SHOWS

Home shows and building and remodeling expos are often scheduled in the spring and fall and advertised in local newspapers. The designers, architects, contractors, real estate agents and assorted vendors on site are ready and willing to spend time with you. It's an easy way to find out about services, shop and compare product lines, and pick up valuable information.

TALK TO FAMILY & FRIENDS

Take time to talk to friends and relatives who have recently completed a home project. You'll find they not only love talking about their homes but can also provide a wealth of information about budgets, suppliers, contractors and designers. Don't forget to ask:

- "What do you wish you had done differently?" Although you might love the way a room looks, you may find out the owners feel they made some mistakes.
- "How much did it cost?" Your friends and family are probably willing to share why and where they went over budget, what their architect cost them, or the square foot cost of their project.

Buy A Software Package

If you like using a computer, check out the software programs that help you design a floor plan, select fixtures or furniture, and turn your selections into a 3-D display. Some programs even provide cost and material worksheets that correspond to your design. What better way to experiment with your ideas before approaching a building professional?

Use Professionals Wisely

Establish your own priorities before you involve professionals in the process. Even if you've already decided to work with an architect or interior designer, keep in mind you'll pay for all the time a professional spends to analyze your project requirements and develop a suitable design. Professional time is expensive, especially when you're asking for full designs and specifications for your project. Architects generally charge an hourly rate, a set fee, or a percentage of total project construction costs, starting at a minimum of 5%. Interior designers charge similarly, either an hourly rate or a percentage of project costs. Take control over these costs by being as prepared as possible before calling a design professional.

> The better organized and knowledgeable you are before construction begins, the smoother the work, the lower the cost, and the less stress on you.

Start A Wishlist

Once you have organized and reviewed all the information you've collected, you're ready to start defining your project by creating a Wishlist. You may think the Wishlist is an unnecessary exercise, but your Wishlist is actually one of the most important places to begin. It not only gives you a starting point for your immediate project, but also forms a plan for future ones as well. As you work through the building process, you'll continue refining this list and will use the information from it to make design and budget decisions.

Use the WISHLIST worksheet to write down everything you would like to include in your new space, regardless of how much it costs. Be creative and note as many details as possible. At this point, you really don't know what the total project is going to cost, so don't limit yourself by omitting items you think you can't afford.

It often helps to stand in the space you are planning to redo and picture the space empty. Think about how you will use your new room. Consider the type of furniture you will put there. Then let your imagination do the rest!

ASK YOURSELF THESE QUESTIONS:

If remodeling the KITCHEN:

- Would I like to change the size of the room?
- Do I want a door that leads out to a deck?
- Would I choose skylights or bay windows?
- Do I want new cabinets?
- Is it time to purchase new appliances?
- Do I need new lighting or additional counter outlets?
- Will I paint or wallpaper?
- What kind of flooring will I buy? Tile, wood, or vinyl?

If remodeling the BATH:

- Should I expand into an adjoining bedroom or closet?
- Could I use double sinks or vanities?
- Would I prefer a separate shower stall?
- Do I want tile on the floor?
- Will I need a larger linen closet?

If adding a FAMILY ROOM:

- Will I use this as my office?
- Do I need some built-ins?
- Will the kids store their toys here?
- How many people will this room accommodate?
- Do I want easy access to the outdoors?
- Do I have enough wall space for my furniture?

 WORKSHEET INSTRUCTIONS

Use the WISHLIST worksheet to describe your design requirements, providing as much detail as possible. If you are remodeling or adding more than one room, create a separate Wishlist for each room.

Start by listing the design elements you want. These might include:

- skylights
- fireplace
- kitchen island
- hot tub
- vaulted ceiling
- walk-in closets

- french doors
- hardwood flooring
- bedroom sitting area
- built-in bookshelves
- new kitchen cabinets
- recessed lighting

Then list any specific products you've found that fit into your plan. For example, if you would like to include a skylight, list "skylight" as one of your design ideas. If you know the specific skylight you'd like to use, write down the manufacturer and model number in the product section of the worksheet.

Note: There are many other uses for the Wishlist worksheet. If, for example, you are planning to purchase an existing home, use this worksheet as a starting place for listing all the features you would like to find in your home. If you've located a house to buy that needs work, use this worksheet to prepare for the remodeling projects that are sure to come.

WISHLIST WORKSHEET

Room: ——————————————— **Room Size:** ———————————————

Design ideas I'd love to include:

———————————————— ————————————————

———————————————— ————————————————

———————————————— ————————————————

———————————————— ————————————————

———————————————— ————————————————

———————————————— ————————————————

———————————————— ————————————————

———————————————— ————————————————

———————————————— ————————————————

Specific products I want to include: (Refer to your notebook and list products
wherever possible.)

———————————————— ————————————————

———————————————— ————————————————

———————————————— ————————————————

———————————————— ————————————————

———————————————— ————————————————

DEFINE YOUR SPACE REQUIREMENTS

One of the decisions you will be making is the size of the space to add or change. Remodeling existing space is most often priced by calculating labor and materials, while the cost of adding new space is determined by price per square foot. In general, the larger your addition, the greater the cost. Later sections in this workbook discuss cutting costs by evaluating desired square footage. However, for the Wishlist, you only need to have a rough idea of the future size of your room.

If you are re-doing an existing room or expanding one room into another, measure the room(s) and mark the information at the top of your Wishlist. If you are adding a new room, you will have to determine the size that you prefer as your starting point. You can get an idea of where to start by measuring some of the rooms in your home.

Here are some suggested minimum sizes when designing a room. Use them as a reference for determining minimum, workable room size. The chart is most useful as a planning guide. It will help you decide whether you are able to squeeze in a bath or powder room or a home office. You will, however, be more comfortable if you can allow for more space than the minimums listed.

MINIMUM WORKABLE ROOM SIZES

ROOM	MINIMUM DIMENSIONS	TOTAL SQUARE FEET
Bathrooms	5' x 8'	40 sq ft
Bedrooms	10' x 11	110 sq ft
Den or Office	8' x 10'	80 sq ft
Family Room	10' x 10'	100 sq ft
Kitchen	8' x 11'	88 sq ft
Eating Area	8' x 8'	64 sq ft
Dining Room	8' x 11'	88 sq ft
Living Room	11' x 14'	154 sq ft
Laundry Area	3' x 5'	15 sq ft
Powder Room	4' x 6'	24 sq ft

PRELIMINARY DESIGN CONCEPTS

Drawing some rough sketches of your plan will help clarify the space requirements for different design concepts you may be considering. The sketches you create will prove useful when you make return visits to showrooms, talk further to salespeople, or meet with designers and contractors. In order for others to provide useful guidance, they will need to know the exact conditions of your existing space.

Keep several copies of your drawings so you can try alternate design ideas.

As you lay out your project, use the following information to guide you:

- Hallways should be a minimum of 36" wide.
- Doorways should have a minimum width of 32".
- Toilets require a minimum of 15" clearance on each side to the center of the seat.
- Vanity sinks require a minimum of 2" from the edge of the sink to a wall or similar obstruction. Double vanity sinks require a 4" separation.
- In front of a vanity or fixture, allow 21" of clearance space.
- Clothes closets should be 28" deep.
- Electric outlets and switches need to be placed out of reach of tubs or showers.
- Windows placed in bedrooms need to be large enough to allow for emergency exit.

WORKSHEET INSTRUCTIONS

There are two worksheets provided: one for your existing layout and one for your new plan. These drawings don't need to be complicated, but should be drawn to scale (in proportion). It's important to take the time to measure your existing space carefully because these measurements will tell you what fixtures or furnishings can actually fit into your room.

Start by measuring the space. Now draw an outline of the floor plan and make sure it is large enough to put in your room's details. The graph sheet allows you one square for each foot (1 ft) you are measuring (e.g., 10 foot wall = 10 squares). After you have drawn the basic room shape, mark in the dimensions for all the walls. Then note the location and measurements of doorways, arches and windows. Draw in wall jogs and closet areas. Finally, sketch in the location of your kitchen cabinets and appliances, bathroom fixtures, or anything that will give a clear picture of your room as it is today. Once these are drawn, note their measurements on the drawing.

When you've completed the sketch of your existing space, draw a second sketch showing your new plan. Start with the overall dimensions of the space then insert the details, just as you did in the first drawing. Measure any special pieces of furniture and art and make a note to allow enough wall space. If you are updating a kitchen, be sure to measure the appliances.

If you are adding a new room entirely, use the "sketch of existing layout" worksheet to show where your new addition will join your existing rooms.

NOTES: MEASUREMENTS (E.G., OF ROOMS, FURNITURE, APPLIANCES)

_____

_____

_____

_____

_____

_____

_____

_____

_____

_____

_____

_____

_____

_____

_____

_____

_____

SKETCH OF EXISTING LAYOUT WORKSHEET

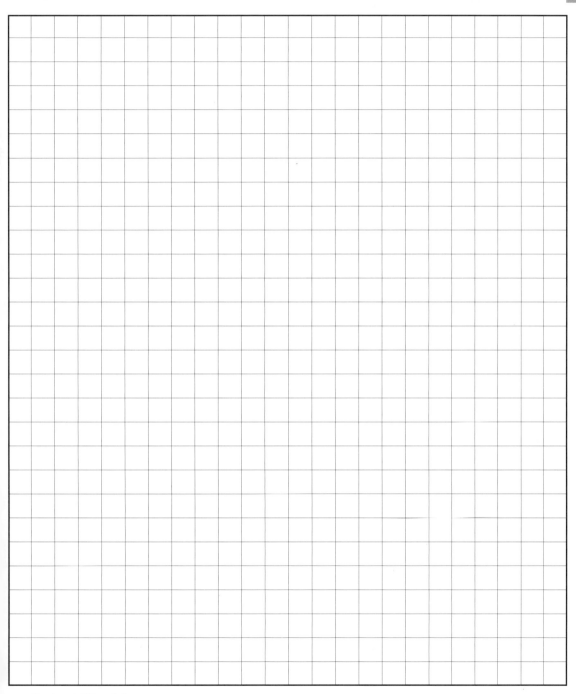

Scale 1/4″ = 1 ft

NOTES: MEASUREMENTS (E.G., OF ROOMS, FURNITURE, APPLIANCES)

_____

_____

_____

_____

_____

_____

_____

_____

_____

_____

_____

_____

_____

_____

_____

_____

_____

_____

_____

Sketch of New Plan Worksheet ————————————

Scale 1/4″ = 1 ft

TIPS: PLANNING & DESIGN

- ❏ Plan appliances before you begin designing your kitchen.

- ❏ Building up is less costly than building out.

- ❏ Design plumbing so that bathrooms are over each other or back to back.

- ❏ Planning early allows you to take advantage of sales on electric fixtures and flooring.

- ❏ Select all kitchen and bath products early to avoid costly delays.

- ❏ Plan switches, outlets and phone locations carefully. Changing locations can be very expensive.

- ❏ Rough in areas for future baths and powder rooms now to save cost and mess in the future.

- ❏ Plan for adequate lighting.

- ❏ Plan door swings to avoid obstructing traffic flow.

- ❏ A skylight offers an alternative where windows are impractical.

- ❏ Pocket doors provide an alternative where you have limited space for door swings.

- ❏ Changes to kitchen and baths are costly to make. Planning now is essential.

Determine Realistic Costs

Your preliminary budget reflects the amount of money you choose to spend on your project. Although you are a long way from having final costs in hand, it's essential at this point to give yourself a general idea of what your project could cost. Drafting a preliminary budget will help you decide whether to go on with your project and will focus you on your home improvement priorities.

No two individuals approach a project the same way. Their tastes and styles will differ, as will their comfort levels when it comes to spending money. If two homeowners with the same financial resources remodel their kitchens, one might spend $10,000 and the other $50,000. The difference in price comes from the specific design and product choices each one makes. Since building costs swing from approximately $60/square foot to over $100/square foot, you first need to understand the price range for the work you want done, then decide where you want your project to fit within the range in order to make informed budget and design decisions.

> Establishing a budget is more than just determining how much money you have in the bank. You'll need to understand what dollar range is realistic for the work you want done, whether the costs make sense in your circumstances, and where you'll find the funds.

You've already gotten some idea of costs by gathering information, window shopping and talking to friends and family. If you need additional information, go to the public library and find The Means Building Construction Cost Data, a book that describes home improvement costs by geographic region. It is a valuable reference tool especially if you are trying to choose between multiple projects based on the funds you have available. Also check out remodeling magazines because they often publish charts showing typical home improvement projects and average costs.

Good budget planning allows a 15% contingency to cover unexpected costs.

Unfortunately, many homeowners start their projects with unrealistic expectations of what it will cost. They then feel pressured and trapped when reality hits. There are many things that can be done to cut expenses and save money, but those decisions need to be made before construction begins. Start off right by developing a realistic picture of costs and build in a comfortable contingency figure to cover surprises. Surprises do happen, especially when remodeling, and it's smart to prepare in advance.

INVESTIGATE HOUSING VALUES

Once you've determined the average price range for your specific type of building/remodeling job, you need to decide how much money is sensible to invest in your home.

If you don't already know the housing values in your neighborhood, investigate them. You want to improve and add value to your home, but ideally you don't want to overprice it for the neighborhood. If homes in the area sell for $200,000 and yours is valued at $150,000, you can safely invest $50,000 into home remodeling projects with an expectation that you will recoup some of your investment if you later sell the property. If your home's value already equals the top-priced homes around you, but you still want to upgrade, recognize that you may not get back the dollars spent on remodeling when you sell.

Determining housing value is also important for individuals planning to purchase a house. If you are looking at existing homes, you can assume there will be some remodeling projects in your future. You'll want to understand the potential costs of future projects so that you can calculate the home's true purchase price. If you've found the "perfect" starter home at a "great" price, but you have to modernize the kitchen, remodel the bath, and/or add a family room to accommodate your lifestyle, perhaps it's not so "perfect" after all. Creating a livable environment might require remodeling costs that are unreasonable when you consider property values in your neighborhood.

Some improvements add perceived value to a home and give you a good return on your money, while others do not. A new master bedroom suite or home office might be just what you need but of little interest or value to someone else. Updates to kitchens and baths generally add value, while basement rec rooms or attic guest rooms do not. The most practical investments are those that improve your home's functionality because they generally provide the best return for your money. Repairing leaky roofs or drafty windows, adding insulation or updating mechanical systems (e.g., heating, plumbing, electrical) are all examples of functional improvements.

While resale and investment value are important factors to consider, so is your desire to improve the quality of your home and create something that's right for you. If you want to add more personalized improvements, go ahead. The object here is to be sensible as you decide how much money to invest in any type remodeling project.

You can get information about housing values in your area by:

- Searching local newspaper listings of recently sold houses, which typically include their selling prices.
- Reading the real estate classified ads to see the asking prices for homes in your area.
- Consulting a realtor. Realtors have access to "comparables", which are computerized printouts of similar houses, their asking and sales prices, and specific information on square footage and special features.

> As you develop your budget, try to balance your personal requirements with the potential investment value of your home improvement.

FINANCING OPTIONS

To establish a useful preliminary budget, you also have to find out how much money you have available for your project. You certainly don't want to start a project only to find out that you're short of money to complete it.

Analyze all the financial avenues open to you. If you are tackling an improvement project costing less than $10,000, you may want to pay with cash from savings. If you are planning a larger project, you may choose to pay some small project expenses with cash. Most home-owners borrow the money they need and there are a number of financing options available.

The two most popular ways to finance a remodeling/building project are:

Home Equity Loan - This type of loan allows you to borrow against the value of your home. Equity is the difference between what your home is worth and the current balance on your mortgage. For example, if your home is worth $150,000 and the mortgage balance is $100,000, there is $50,000 worth of equity in your home. Since banks typically lend 80% of the equity amount, you would be able to obtain a $40,000 home equity loan. Many home equity loans are structured as lines of credit, allowing you to draw funds as you need them. Since you pay interest on the money only as you borrow it, this can be an inexpensive way to borrow.

Refinancing Your Mortgage - When you refinance your mortgage, you obtain a new mortgage and pay off the old one. Most banks will lend between 75%-80% of the appraised value of a home, which allows you to use any monies you receive above your existing mortgage for remodeling. Refinancing makes sense when the interest rate for the new mortgage is lower than the interest rate you are currently paying, or when your existing mortgage balance is small. When mortgage interest rates are low, refinancing your mortgage can be one of the most cost-effective ways to borrow money. Refinancing does not make sense if you already have a low-interest mortgage or when you have little equity. A new mortgage will usually have a lower interest rate than a home equity loan, but the up-front costs of a mortgage will be higher.

There are other, less popular ways to finance home improvements including home improvement loans, personal loans, and loans offered by remodeling companies. Check these options out carefully as they have higher interest rates and shorter terms than either a new mortgage or a home equity line of credit.

There is one word to remember when it comes to using credit cards to finance your home improvement project - DON'T. Credit card rates are so high that you should limit credit card purchases to small ticket items only.

How Much Can You Borrow?

Lenders determine the amount you can borrow based on your gross income, existing debt and credit history. Your lender decides how much debt you can handle. In general, lenders do not want you to spend more than 28% of your gross monthly income to cover total house payments, or more than 36% of your gross monthly income to cover all your fixed monthly expenses, including mortgage payments, loans and credit card payments. The actual percentages vary depending on the institution. Lenders can adjust these ratios after they analyze your total financial situation, including credit history, source of income and savings.

The following table illustrates the formula banks use to establish mortgage payment, based on a borrower's gross monthly income. The table shows, for example, if your gross monthly income is $2,000, your monthly mortgage payment (principal, interest, taxes, insurance) should not exceed $560 and your total monthly expenses should not exceed $720. Use the information in the chart only as a guide as some programs allow higher ratios.

LENDING RATIOS

GROSS MONTHLY INCOME	MAXIMUM MONTHLY MORTGAGE PAYMENT	MAXIMUM TOTAL MONTHLY INSTALLMENT DEBT
	28%	36%
$ 1,000	$ 280	$ 360
1,100	308	396
1,200	336	432
1,300	364	468
1,400	392	504
1,500	420	540
1,600	448	576
1,700	476	612
1,800	504	648
1,900	532	684
2,000	560	720
2,100	588	756
2,200	616	792
2,300	644	828
2,400	672	864
2,500	700	900
2,600	728	936
2,700	756	972
2,800	784	1008
2,900	812	1044
3,000	840	1080
3,100	868	1116
3,200	896	1152
3,300	924	1188
3,400	952	1224
3,500	980	1260

WORKSHEET INSTRUCTIONS

The FINANCIAL worksheet helps you prepare the information a lender will require when you apply for a loan. It does take time to compile all the details, but by doing so you will be ready to provide them, as required, when you make your loan application. By putting in the effort now, you'll cut the time it typically takes to complete the loan process.

Collect the following records for each person applying:

- tax returns and W-2 forms for the past two years
- current pay stubs
- information on credit card debt, student loans, car loans and other loans you owe
- current statements for checking and savings accounts
- recent statements for mutual funds, stock accounts, or other investments
- if self-employed, provide a current year-to-date statement of income and expenses.

Fill in the Monthly Income section noting all of your income sources. Next, work on calculating your total monthly expenses. Monthly expenses include car and credit card payments, student or other types of loans, but not your current housing payment. You do not have to list your credit cards if you pay off the balances every month.

Lenders will also want to know what assets you own that would enable you to pay off a loan, so you need to compile the information for the Savings and Assets section of the worksheet.

After you've completed the Financial worksheet, review the Lending Ratio Table. It will give you an indication of how a lender will evaluate your ability to qualify for a loan.

FINANCIAL WORKSHEET

MONTHLY INCOME

Gross Monthly Income   _____

Commissions   _____

Bonuses   _____

Dividend/Interest Income   _____

Business/Investment Income   _____

Pensions/Social Security   _____

Alimony/Child Support   _____

Rental Income   _____

TOTAL MONTHLY INCOME $ _____

MONTHLY EXPENSES	Current Balance Owed	Monthly Payment
Car Payment	_____	_____
Student Loans	_____	_____
Medical Payments	_____	_____
Credit Cards:		
name _____		
acct # _____	_____	_____
name _____		
acct # _____	_____	_____
name _____		
acct # _____	_____	_____
name _____		
acct # _____	_____	_____

	Current Balance Owed	Monthly Payment
name _____	_____	_____
acct# _____	_____	_____
Alimony/Child Support	_____	_____
Other	_____	_____
Other	_____	_____

TOTAL MONTHLY INCOME $ _____

SAVINGS/ASSETS: Cash or Market Value

Bank Accounts

name _____	acct # _____	_____
name _____	acct # _____	_____
name _____	acct # _____	_____

Brokerage Accounts

name _____	acct# _____	_____
name _____	acct # _____	_____

Stocks & Bonds	_____
Life Insurance Cash Value	_____
Real Estate Owned	_____
Other	_____

The Preliminary Budget

Once you have a good sense of what your type of project might cost and what you want to spend, you can create a preliminary budget. Control over project costs begins by deciding what is to be included in your workplan and establishing a budget for this work. Setting a budget will allow you to keep track of costs as you make your selections and bid the job. When you get actual price quotes for the work, you'll be able to compare these quotes to your preliminary budget and get an accurate picture of where you stand financially. You'll also be able to make adjustments to design and products before you finalize your plans. Trying to adjust your budget during construction results in confusion and delays to your job. The time to make changes in your workplan is well before construction starts.

The most important way to keep project costs within your control is to create a budget and follow it.

WORKSHEET INSTRUCTIONS

The PRELIMINARY COSTS worksheet is the starting point for the budget decisions you will be making. To complete it, you will want to review your Wishlist.

In the worksheet's left column, write in the items from your Wishlist. To fill in the projected costs in the right column, use the information you've collected regarding pricing. If you don't know an exact price, fill in a price range for the product or work to be done. Before going any further in the process, you should have a realistic idea of what each Wishlist item will cost.

In order to get a complete picture of project costs, add 15% as a contingency for unexpected expenses and 5% for any professional fees you might incur.

NOTES: PRODUCTS & PRICES

_____

_____

_____

_____

_____

_____

_____

_____

_____

_____

_____

_____

_____

_____

PRELIMINARY COSTS WORKSHEET

STEP 2

WISHLIST ITEM	PROJECTED COST
1. _____	_____
2. _____	_____
3. _____	_____
4. _____	_____
5. _____	_____
6. _____	_____
7. _____	_____
8. _____	_____
9. _____	_____
10. _____	_____
11. _____	_____
12. _____	_____
13. _____	_____
14. _____	_____
15. _____	_____
16. _____	_____
17. _____	_____
18. _____	_____
19. _____	_____
20. _____	_____

WISHLIST ITEM	PROJECTED COST
21. _____	_____
22. _____	_____
23. _____	_____
24. _____	_____
25. _____	_____
26. _____	_____
27. _____	_____
28. _____	_____
29. _____	_____
30. _____	_____

Subtotal $ _____

Contingencies @15% $ _____

Professional Fees @ 5% $ _____

TOTAL $ _____

ESTABLISH PRIORITIES

With your preliminary budget in mind, review and clarify your remodeling goals. Figure out which items on your Wishlist are priorities and which are "extras" to be included if your budget permits. Once you receive actual building/remodeling estimates, you'll be better able to evaluate your ability to include these extras.

Prioritizing your Wishlist creates a master plan for remodeling and ensures that the most important items on your list get done.

WORKSHEET INSTRUCTIONS

Use the PROJECT PRIORITIES worksheet to rank the items on your Wishlist. Organize your list into "must haves" and work your way, in order of importance, to the items that would be "nice to have".

Top priorities should be the items that are either "structural" in nature or that would be disruptive to accomplish after your remodeling is complete. These elements should be done before cosmetic or "finish" items that could be installed or upgraded in the future with minimal disruption.

Here are some suggestions:

Consider doing now:

- framing
- windows & exterior doors
- fireplace
- wall insulation
- skylights

Can be delayed:

- hardwood flooring
- new sinks & faucets
- new countertops
- new lighting fixtures
- wallpaper

Consider doing now:	Can be delayed:

Consider doing now:

- altering room size
- anything recessed or built-in
- cabinets
- wiring, plumbing or heating for future rooms

Can be delayed:

- interior doors
- closet organizers
- special trims & moldings
- decks & patios

Perhaps you're planning a kitchen addition and envision a large, country kitchen with attached family room, a bay window, hardwood floors, new cabinets and appliances. Decide what you *need* to accomplish vs. what you'd *like* to accomplish. Rank all items with a number, starting with the most important and continuing through the least important design element.

NOTES: NEEDS & WANTS

_____

_____

_____

_____

_____

_____

_____

_____

_____

_____

_____

_____

_____

PROJECT PRIORITIES WORKSHEET

MUST HAVE	NICE TO HAVE
1. _____	16. _____
2. _____	17. _____
3. _____	18. _____
4. _____	19. _____
5. _____	20. _____
6. _____	21. _____
7. _____	22. _____
8. _____	23. _____
9. _____	24. _____
10. _____	25. _____
11. _____	26. _____
12. _____	27. _____
13. _____	28. _____
14. _____	29. _____
15. _____	30. _____

Consider this list your master plan as you approach your project. By distinguishing your needs from your wants, you can stage your remodeling and work within your budget.

LIST OF ACCOMPLISHMENTS

Let's review the steps you've taken so far. You have:

- Gathered enough information to define your project and establish realistic budget parameters by window shopping, visiting product showrooms, and talking to people who recently completed remodeling projects.
- Completed a rough sketch of your initial plan.
- Decided the total amount of money you want to spend by balancing investment value and personal circumstances and preferences.
- Coordinated and verified your project funding source(s).
- Established clear priorities for the project.

Congratulations! With these tasks accomplished, you've created a solid foundation on which to build the all-important details of your plan. Of course, you'll still be refining your ideas and testing your budget in the marketplace, but you've established basic guidelines before bringing professionals into the decision-making process.

If you are confused at this point or your accomplishments don't match the ones on the list, go back and review all the information you've collected. Reconsider your project and your budget until you are satisfied that you have a realistic and clear vision. Without it, you are only setting yourself up for disappointment.

TIPS: SMART BUDGETING

❏ Kitchens and baths provide the greatest return on investment when you sell your home.

❏ Bathroom accessories (e.g., mirrors, towel bars and toilet paper holders) are commonly forgotten but should be included in your budget.

❏ Use products of standard measurements to avoid the cost of special orders.

❏ Investigate different plumbing fixture products carefully. Prices vary greatly.

❏ Over insulating your home is not cost effective.

❏ Steel and fiberglass exterior doors are an economical alternative to wood doors and are maintenance free.

❏ Molded interior doors give the look of wood doors but are considerably less expensive.

❏ Hardwood flooring is available at prices that vary widely. Spend some time investigating your options.

❏ Buy good quality paint. The cost of paint is a fraction of the labor.

❏ Don't forget to allow for window treatments in your budget.

❏ To cut costs, install carpeting now and replace it with hardwood or tile later when you can afford to do the work.

❏ Select items available from local suppliers to avoid having to custom order.

❏ Built-ins may be an economical alternative to purchasing furniture.

❏ A fireplace installed on the inside of your house is far less costly than a masonry fireplace built on the outside. Investigate "drop-in" wood or gas fireplaces.

Prepare A Description of Your Plan

Your next step is to create a set of drawings and specifications that you can use to get project estimates. Specifications (specs) are nothing more than a description of all the details, materials and products to be used in the execution of your project. Once you have finalized your plans, everyone involved in your project will refer to these drawings and specs as work is done. You can either create them yourself or hire a professional designer. If you are planning to hire a professional designer (e.g., architect, interior designer, engineer) to assist you with your project's design and provide project drawings, you can turn to the same professional to create the specifications needed to bid the project.

PERMITS & REGULATIONS

You will also use your drawings and specs when you go to the city or town building department for a building permit. If you are building an addition or doing a project involving structural modifications to an existing home, you will be required to provide drawings that show the technical details of your construction. Structural changes are those that affect your home's ability to remain solidly in position over time. Examples of structural changes include lifting a roof to create a new room, relocating load-bearing walls or putting on an addition. "Stamped" drawings, provided by a licensed architect or engineer, are required for all new construction or remodeling projects involving structural changes. The "stamp" refers to the architect's or engineer's seal which is stamped on the plans and then signed. The purpose of stamping drawings is to guarantee that a project has structural integrity. Because of the liability involved, architects or engineers will not stamp someone else's drawings.

Many homeowners would like to avoid getting a building permit because they believe that the permit requirement will translate into an increase in their property taxes. Although this is sometimes true, it is important to realize that the permit process also protects you from potential health and safety building violations. The construction inspections that are built into the building permit process are your assurance that the work your contractor performs meets minimum building codes. These inspections are designed for your protection and not your harassment. Note, though, that permit inspections are for code items and do not set standards of quality for your construction. The issue of quality remains between you and your contractor.

If you are building an addition, you will also have to provide a plot or site plan showing the "footprint" of your home on your lot. An architect or engineer can provide this drawing.

Find out about local building, zoning and planning ordinances, the paperwork your municipality requires, and the deadlines you must meet in order to get the necessary approvals for a building permit.

All municipalities have zoning regulations that address matters relating to what can be built in a specific location, the size of a building in relation to lot size, and the distance required between lot lines and any building structure, including decks and patios. In neighborhoods that have been designated as historic, there will be additional requirements to ensure that all houses maintain the historic flavor of the area.

For small projects, building departments may only require a simple drawing indicating your layout, window placement and sizes, and types of fixtures being used. Bath and kitchen remodeling projects that don't involve structural changes do not require stamped drawings. If this is your situation, you can provide your own drawings if you are comfortable taking on the task.

WORKSHEET INSTRUCTIONS

If you are supplying your own drawings, use the PROJECT DRAWING worksheet to prepare a neat, scaled drawing clearly showing the design layout of your project. Refer back to the sketches you originally drew. Add whatever details are necessary to show the final layout of your new plan. You will also need to provide the drawing of your existing space to show that no structural changes are to be made. If you need additional help with these drawings, you can find floor plan kits at building supply and hardware stores or innovative software programs that generate drawings, ranging from simple line drawings of layout to professional looking blueprints.

PROJECT DRAWING WORKSHEET

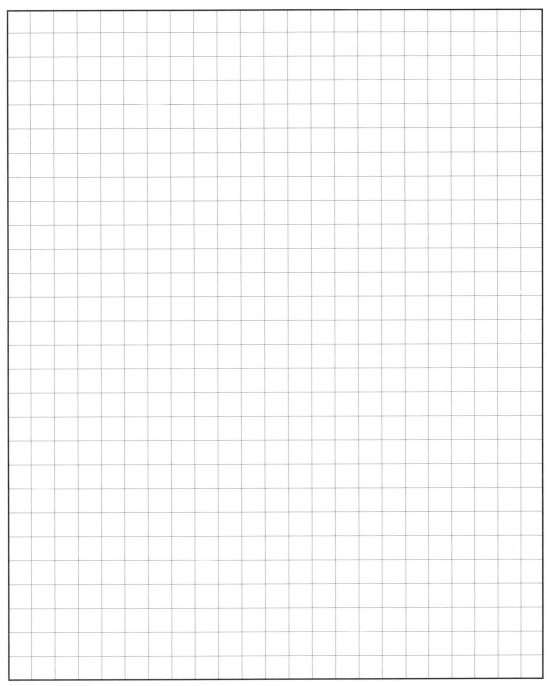

Scale   1/4″ = 1 ft

PROFESSIONAL HELP

Regardless of your project size, you may want to get professional help with your layout and design and have the same professional prepare a project drawing. Professional designers have the training, knowledge and experience to help you refine your ideas, solve layout problems, meet zoning and building code requirements, and take you through the construction process. They can be tremendously helpful in suggesting alternatives that will dramatically improve your project. Make sure, though, that you have targeted your own design and budget goals prior to seeking help from a professional.

One of the first places people get in trouble budget-wise is by asking professionals to get involved too early. All too often, homeowners approach a designer for assistance before thinking through or agreeing on the goals for their project. They let the designer define their Wishlist, get excited with the wonderful design suggestions presented to them, have drawings created, send the package to bid, and then find that the cost estimates come in far beyond their expectations or budget. These homeowners are forced to re-think their project and spend more time and money on new drawings. This experience is not only disappointing but very costly. Spend your time and money wisely by having a clear idea of your needs and wants so you can use the creativity of the designer to enhance - rather than define - your design concepts. No matter what your personal circumstances are, never present your project design and budget as open-ended.

> To get the most value from professional help, give every professional with whom you'll be working a clearly defined concept of what you are trying to achieve for the price you are willing to pay.

TYPES OF DESIGNERS

You have several types of design professionals from which to choose. Each has a different level of training and provides somewhat different services.

Architects are trained and licensed to manage all aspects of a building project. Many architects, however, don't design small remodeling projects. If you need an architect and aren't sure which ones will work on smaller residential projects, call your local chapter of the American Institute of Architects (AIA) and ask for referrals. Architects will either charge a set fee, work on hourly rates, charge a percentage of your construction budget, or any combination of the three, depending on the scope of work involved.

A <u>Draftsperson</u> is able to draw plans, but is not licensed to do any design or structural work. A draftsperson is usually associated with an architectural or engineering firm and may be a good resource to provide drawings for a relatively simple project that doesn't involve structural changes.

<u>Independent Home Designers</u> are not licensed, but may have some training in interior design, drawing and managing building projects. Most of the larger retail building supply stores and kitchen and bath showrooms have their own independent designers, who advise shoppers on home projects and sell the stores' products. These designers will often provide drawings if you purchase your materials at their store. In some cases, you may be able to buy any drawings they've completed for your project even if you ultimately decide to go elsewhere for materials.

<u>Design/Build Contracting Businesses</u> have recently become the place for one-stop shopping for home remodeling projects. These businesses employ both designers and contractors and can provide design ideas, blueprints and contractors to do your work. While hiring such a business makes it easy for you to get through the planning stage of your project, you give up the ability to check out competitive prices and alternative design ideas. Bottom line - you get only one perspective and one project price.

The same holds true for <u>Individual Contractors</u>. A contractor can provide drawings of your project and very often is the best one to do so, particularly for small remodeling projects. Recognize, however, that contractors are not trained in design and that some contractors are more creative than others. If you use a contractor for both design ideas and building cost estimates, you are left, as with the design/build companies, with only one viewpoint and one bid. You lose the checks and balances inherent in involving different professionals throughout the planning process. If you plan to have a contractor supply any drawings required for your building permit, first create your own sketches and specifications to get project estimates and select a contractor. Once you've found the right contractor for your job, you can have him supply any refined drawings you may need.

<u>Interior Decorators</u> determine how a room will be furnished and decorated. Their skill lies in their ability to organize furniture and accessories, select colors and wallcoverings, and essentially bring life to an empty space. Their decisions can affect the type and location of windows and doors, placement of recessed lighting and use of built-in cabinets. Interior designers are not, however, experts in construction. Used in tandem with the other designers, a good decorator can greatly enhance your finished product.

How To Choose A Designer

Look for a designer with whom you can communicate and are comfortable. You want someone who will be able to provide technical expertise and guidance with your project goals in mind. Find someone who has an eye on costs and can suggest alternatives that save you money. A good designer will help you express your own vision. Use a designer to fill in the gaps in your knowledge and assist you in the areas where you need help. Remember that you are buying his or her expertise and paying for time spent on your project.

In your enthusiasm, its easy to fall into the trap of thinking that everyone is as concerned about your project as you are. The reality is that while you are focusing on your project in a very personal way, everyone else is involved because they do this work for a living. Your project is just one of many they are being paid to do. This is your project, so be watchful and stay alert. Pay attention to the details in order to get what you want!

Arrange initial meetings with design professionals to evaluate which professional is right for you. At these meetings *briefly* describe your project and budget goals. Find out if they have done similar projects within the past year and if your time frame fits into their schedules. Ask each:

- to explain his or her procedures
- when you will be presented with sketches for approval
- about fee structures and related costs
- who you'll be working with throughout the process

Finally, ask for at least three client references.

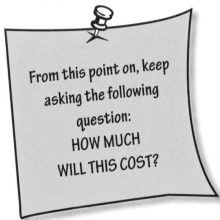

From this point on, keep asking the following question:
HOW MUCH
WILL THIS COST?

WORKSHEET INSTRUCTIONS

The DESIGNERS REFERENCE worksheet suggests those things to be considered as you search for a designer. It's very important that you feel comfortable with whomever you choose and that you not be intimidated by his or her expertise. You want to be able to exchange ideas freely and veto suggestions that fall outside your design or budget parameters. By asking for client references (and calling those references), you will get an idea of the working relationship you can expect to develop with a particular designer. To get a fair assessment, call more than one reference and listen carefully to what they tell you.

Once you've decided on a designer, use the sketches and materials in your project notebook to communicate your ideas. Take your time during the design phase because it is important to plan and explore concepts thoroughly. Keep stating your goal to keep the design within your budget. When you emphasize your budget, you remind the designer to search for alternative design solutions. Try to get a cost estimate for your plan as soon as possible. Once you have a more refined list of project costs, you'll be better able to judge how many of your Wishlist items you can continue to include.

NOTES: NAMES OF DESIGNERS & PHONE NUMBERS

_____

_____

_____

_____

_____

_____

STEP 3

DESIGNERS REFERENCES WORKSHEET

Client: _____

Phone: _____

Type of project: _____

Client: _____

Phone: _____

Type of project: _____

Client: _____

Phone: _____

Type of project: _____

QUESTIONS TO ASK:

1. Was (s)he creative and good at problem solving?

_____

_____

_____

2. Did (s)he keep your goals and concerns in mind?

_____

_____

_____

3. Was (s)he easy to work with?

_____

_____

_____

4. Were your drawings complete and satisfactory to your contractor?

_____

_____

_____

5. Were there any problems that specifically arose from the design?

_____

_____

_____

6. Were his/her initial price estimates accurate? Did your project come in on budget?

_____

_____

_____

7. Did (s)he meet deadlines?

_____

_____

_____

8. Was there anything about your project that could have been done better?

_____

_____

_____

The Importance of Specifications

One option you may want to consider is using a designer to help with layout and draw your plans, but preparing the written specifications yourself. Building permit requirements may dictate that you have professional drawings to detail structural elements, but the same does not hold true for specs. It isn't necessary to have a designer complete a detailed set of specs for your entire project, and, in fact, most home improvement projects do not use professional specifications.

In order to create project specs, you'll first have to make some product decisions. Choosing products is necessary in order to prepare an accurate description of your project. Because contractors work on so many different projects with a range of clients and budgets, you must tell them specifically what you want in order to get a realistic estimate for your job. It's a waste of time to call a contractor for a cost estimate before you decide on your design or the types of products you'd like used. A 500 square foot addition could cost $30,000 or $60,000 depending on the types of products you select. Failing to give a contractor enough information is precisely how homeowners develop unrealistic perceptions of cost. The clearer you are about design and products, the more relevant the bids will be.

Avoid This Common Mistake

All too often, a homeowner gets estimates by walking through his home with a contractor, having a conversation about what he wants done. The homeowner talks, the contractor offers some suggestions then goes off to prepare his or her bid. When the next contractor arrives the process is repeated. When the homeowner receives the bids, he is confused and surprised by the wide range of quotes for the "same" job.

Why were the bids so different? It's quite simple. While the homeowner thought he was explaining his project clearly, he failed to follow a very important rule: *To get useful bids, the description of your project needs to be specific and in writing!* If you are not specific when getting estimates, the quotes you receive will only reflect each contractor's *perception* of your job.

WRITTEN SPECS PREVENT PROBLEMS

Written specs help you communicate what you want, allow all the contractors to bid the same work, and alleviate many misunderstandings between contractor and homeowner during the course of construction. No matter the size of your project, written specs tell all contractors exactly what you want done and the materials you want used. In larger projects, specs provide the details not found in your drawings. In more straightforward jobs that require no drawings, written specs are necessary to ensure consistent bids.

Written specifications are essential to getting useful bids. They clearly communicate to all contractors exactly what you want done and what materials you want used.

What if you don't have any idea of all that's involved in your job or you're unsure of the materials you want used? Lets say, for example, that you want to have the exterior of your home painted. You can still create written specs by doing one of the following:

Option A:

1. Take a trip to the paint store and talk to a salesperson about your project.
2. Select the type of paint you think you might want to use.
3. Write up a description of what you want done and include the specifics of the paint you've chosen (these are your specs).
4. Call some contractors for bids based on your specs.

Option B:

1. Call a contractor.
2. Get his quote for your job and ask that it be detailed and in writing.
3. Study his quote carefully to understand what is involved.
4. Use the information (but not his price) from his bid to create your specs and get additional bids.

What if you've selected a specific product, but as you speak to different contractors, they suggest something they think would be better? Have the contractors quote what you've requested and their suggestions. This will give you a basis for comparing their prices plus give you the ability to evaluate different approaches to your project.

As you create your project specs, remember that at this point in the process you are not locked into any of the details you include in your specifications. You are just trying to clearly communicate what you'd like done and establishing a standard against which to measure all pricing. You will have plenty of time to make changes to your specs before signing a contract.

WHAT TO INCLUDE IN YOUR SPECS

Your written specifications should include:

1. *All material and product details*: specific manufacturers or brand names, model numbers, colors and sizes where applicable.

>   *Example*:   You are remodeling your bathroom and will need the bathroom painted.

UNCLEAR	CLEAR
paint	paint 2 coats, Benjamin Moore, "Regal Aquaglo" latex semi-gloss enamel, color: China White #74

2. *Responsibilities*: Clarify any part of the job to be done by others, including other contractors, suppliers or yourself. If you have drawings or product information from other tradesmen who will be working on your project, include copies (without the prices) in your specifications. This gives each contractor a complete understanding of what your job entails.

>   *Example*:   You are building a kitchen addition. You have been working with a kitchen supplier on layout and design and have already selected your cabinets. The supplier has told you that the price includes the installation. You've also selected hardwood flooring from another store that will be providing a contractor to install it.

UNCLEAR	CLEAR
new cabinets	new cabinets to be supplied and installed by others-see attached plan
hardwood flooring	1/2" thick hardwood flooring to be supplied and installed by others

3. *Allowances*: An allowance is the dollar amount you allocate to any job category for materials and products you have not yet selected. When you specify an allowance, you are telling the contractor how much money to budget for that category. The contractor is then able to include your allowance in his estimate even though you have not made specific product decisions. This allowance amount becomes the amount of money you are "allowed" to spend when you finally select your products. If the value of the allowance is greater than what's needed to purchase those items, you'll receive a credit from the contractor. If the allowance is less than the items wind up costing, you'll pay the difference.

It's not uncommon to include allowances for lighting fixtures, kitchen cabinets, hardware or flooring in a contract. At the time most people are getting estimates and selecting their contractor, they haven't yet made all their final product decisions. When it comes to allowances, you need to have done enough shopping and pricing to have a reasonably accurate idea of what these items will cost. If you're unsure of their cost you may find yourself having to choose lesser quality products to stay within your contract price, or, worse yet, you may end up with a significant budget deficit.

It is much better for you to set the allowances than to let the contractor set them for you. Some contractors include an allowance amount in their bid that is too low to cover real purchases. They do this to keep their overall bid price low and win the job. When establishing allowance figures, ask yourself, "Is that a reasonable amount of money to purchase what I want?"

Example: You have not yet selected the lighting fixtures for your addition.

UNCLEAR
lighting fixtures
not yet selected

CLEAR
lighting fixture allowance @ $925.00

Because setting allowance amounts can be tricky, you may want to avoid the issue completely by not even including allowances in your specs. You may think that you're better off waiting until you've made final product decisions, then buying those things yourself and supplying them to the job. The problem with that strategy is that a contractor is not responsible for any products you bring to the job. He's only responsible for the products he supplies. In other words, if you give your contractor a faucet you've purchased in your local hardware store and there is a problem after it's installed, he has every right to charge you what it cost to replace the defective faucet with a new one. If, however, the contractor supplied the same defective faucet, he'd be responsible for replacing it at no charge.

If you're uncomfortable specifying allowance amounts, you have an alternative. You can select products that reflect what you might ultimately choose and specify them as your standard of quality.

Example:

UNCLEAR	CLEAR
new vanity sink	Kohler K2931, or equal

4. *Demolition*: This category covers any tear-out or demolition to be done as well as debris removal (which can be surprisingly costly).

5. *Exterior work*: As a result of interior remodeling, you may end up needing exterior repair work. This might include siding repair, exterior painting or landscaping work.

6. *Building Permit*: Identify who will obtain the building permit.

WORKSHEET INSTRUCTIONS

Once you've chosen most of your products, you're ready to complete the SPECIFICATIONS worksheet. Start by reviewing all the notes, pictures, sketches, product and material information you've collected in your notebook. Also review your Priorities worksheet. Then turn to the SPECIFICATIONS worksheet and list the elements of your workplan by referring to your Priorities. The items on your Priorities worksheet are essentially your workplan items.

For example, in re-doing your kitchen, you plan to have new cabinets. One of the items on your Priorities worksheet would be "new cabinets." For the spec worksheet, you expand upon this concept. Who will purchase the cabinets - you or your contractor? Who will install them? Try to envision your project from start to finish, step by step. To help you think through the type of work that's involved in a remodeling project, see Step 7 - Oversee the Work in Progress, and its brief overview of the stages of construction.

After you've filled in the Workplan column of the worksheet, use the corresponding number in the Details column to write a description of each work item or product. Include manufacturer information, model numbers or colors. Use your notebook information for reference. If you look carefully at most product brochures, you will find model numbers or names that correspond to particular items. If you do not have detailed information about a product you're including, call or visit stores to get the information. You can also attach a picture, product sheet or even a material sample to your specs to clearly identify what you want.

Creating your remodeling specs is not difficult. What's more, it is your opportunity to focus on the products you want and imagine the work from start to finish. Don't worry. You will be reviewing your drawings and specs with the contractors bidding your job. If anything remains unclear, you'll discover it in those discussions or when you compare the contractors bids. You still have time to amend your specs before signing a contract.

Here is an example of how you might detail some of the items for a bathroom remodeling job.

WORKPLAN ELEMENTS	DETAILS
1. Remove toilet, sink & faucet, vanity & flooring	1. Contractor will do all demolition & debris removal
2. Supply & install new 48" vanity cabinet & top	2. See attached product sheet
3. Supply & install new toilet	3. Kohler, K3384, color: Mexican Sand
4. Supply & install new sink	4. Kohler K2931, color: Teal
5. Supply & install new faucet	5. Kohler K16102-4 in polished brass
6. Supply & install new vinyl flooring	6. Allowance @ $750.00
7. Paint bathroom	7. 2 coats Benjamin Moore, Regal Aquaglo, latex, semi-gloss, color: White Blush #904
8. Replace 1 electric fixture	8. Fixture to be supplied by owner

AS YOU WRITE YOUR SPECS, MAKE SURE YOU HAVE:

- Checked your worksheets and notes to make sure you have included all basics that can't be added later.
- Prioritized your needs so you know what you can eliminate or postpone.
- Specified brand names of the products you want.
- Defined room sizes.
- Clarified who will be obtaining any required permits.
- Considered any exterior work that might need to be redone resulting from interior work.
- Developed realistic costs for any allowance amounts to be included.
- Included pictures, product sheets or anything that helps clarify the job.

NOTES: SPECIFICATION DETAILS

_____

_____

_____

_____

_____

_____

_____

_____

_____

_____

_____

_____

_____

_____

SPECIFICATIONS WORKSHEET

WORKPLAN	DETAILS
1. _____	1. _____
2. _____	2. _____
3. _____	3. _____
4. _____	4. _____
5. _____	5. _____
6. _____	6. _____
7. _____	7. _____
8. _____	8. _____
9. _____	9. _____
10. _____	10. _____
11. _____	11. _____
12. _____	12. _____
13. _____	13. _____
14. _____	14. _____
15. _____	15. _____
16. _____	16. _____
17. _____	17. _____
18. _____	18. _____
19. _____	19. _____
20. _____	20. _____

STEP 3

WORKPLAN	**DETAILS**
21. _____	21. _____
22. _____	22. _____
23. _____	23. _____
24. _____	24. _____
25. _____	25. _____
26. _____	26. _____
27. _____	27. _____
28. _____	28. _____
29. _____	29. _____
30. _____	30. _____

Miscellaneous: _____

_____

_____

_____

_____

_____

_____

_____

_____

_____

_____

_____

_____

THE BID SHEET

With drawings and specs in hand, you're *almost* ready to find contractors to bid your project. You've prepared all the documents that give the contractors a clear description of your project. All you need now is a Bid Sheet to help you decipher their bids. A Bid Sheet is an invaluable tool for understanding how a contractor arrived at his total price, comparing his price to your preliminary cost projections, and finding areas of negotiation within his bid.

Every contractor seems to have a unique way of presenting a written proposal. When it comes time for you to evaluate the bids, you'll want to be able to compare the costs of similar line items. Many contractors, especially when they are bidding on small remodeling projects, submit a "lump sum" price covering all work to be done. Typically, they give you a proposal that contains no other information than this: "Labor and Materials to complete kitchen addition.....$31,400.00". Unfortunately, this type of bid doesn't give you any indication as to how the contractor arrived at his price. It also doesn't give you a way to fairly compare his bid to others, and most importantly, doesn't provide enough information for you to evaluate the areas where you might save money. Using a Bid Sheet will allow you to:

- more easily compare contractors' prices
- make sure all your job categories were included in each bid
- spot areas where you can negotiate prices
- pinpoint the areas that add cost to your project

WORKSHEET INSTRUCTIONS

The BID SHEET is an outline of categories of work involved in your project. Instead of listing individual tasks and products separately (as in your spec worksheet), it groups them together within broader categories.

Here are some examples of specific tasks/items and the general categories they would fall under:

ELECTRICAL
- new switches & outlets
- installing lighting fixtures, phone jacks, cable, speaker wires
- adding circuits
- stove, oven, microwave, range hood installation
- wiring for dishwashers, washers & dryers

PLUMBING
- replacing a hot water heater
- installing the water line(s) for a dishwasher, washing machine, ice-maker
- replacing sinks, toilets, faucets, shower stalls
- adding an outside hose hook-up

FINISH CARPENTRY
- installing moldings and railings
- hanging closet doors
- replacing door hardware
- installing cabinets & countertops

Depending on the complexity of your project, you can create as many or few categories as you need. Remember that the purpose of the Bid Sheet is to help you compare the different estimates you get. You're free to organize it however you'd like.

The following sample Bid Sheet lists categories you might use if you were building an addition, but it is useful for other types of projects as well. All of the categories may not apply to your project, but they will give you an idea of how to organize your own Bid Sheet. Create a sheet with categories that relate to your specific job, or adapt this one by crossing out the categories that don't apply.

Fill in any allowances and mark as not applicable (NA) the areas where you are hiring other people to complete specific parts of your project.

YOUR BID PACKAGE

Every contractor who will be estimating your job should be given:

- your bid sheet
- a copy of your drawings
- a set of specifications

This will become your bid package. Once this package is complete, you are ready to start the bidding process.

NOTES: BID SHEET

Bid Sheet Worksheet

Contractor: _____

Phone #: _____

1. Demolition & Debris Removal $ _____
2. Excavation _____
3. Concrete & Masonry _____
4. Framing _____
5. Lumber _____
6. Windows & Doors _____
7. Siding _____
8. Roofing _____
9. Gutters _____
10. Landscaping _____
11. Insulation _____
12. Plumbing _____
13. Heating _____
14. Electric _____
15. Drywall _____
16. Finish Carpentry _____
17. Painting _____
18. Cabinets & Counter Tops _____
19. Plumbing Fixtures _____
20. Lighting Fixtures _____
21. Flooring _____
22. Ceramic Tile _____
23. Hardware _____
24. Miscellaneous Conditions _____
25. Specialty Items _____

TOTAL BID $ _____

CHECKLIST FOR PREPARING PLANS AND SPECS

- ❏ Have you found out about local building and zoning codes?
- ❏ Did you interview a number of designers?
- ❏ Do you have a clearly defined concept of your project and budget?
- ❏ Did you check your worksheets and notes to make sure you included all basics that cannot be added later?
- ❏ Did you prioritize your needs so you know what you can eliminate or postpone?
- ❏ Did you specify brand names of products?
- ❏ Have you defined all room sizes?
- ❏ Were you clear as to who will be obtaining any permits?
- ❏ Did you include any exterior work that might need to be done as a result of your interior remodeling?
- ❏ Did you research allowance amounts?
- ❏ Did you prepare a bid sheet?
- ❏ Do you have a complete bid package for every contractor?

How Do I Select the Right Contractor?

Find Reputable Contractors To Bid

At this stage you're working to achieve two very important objectives: 1) to get contractor estimates so you can evaluate your priorities and make final budget decisions, and 2) to determine which contractor is best suited for your job. While these goals are related, the tasks are distinctly different to accomplish.

Contracting can be a strange business. Anyone with some tools and a truck can call himself a contractor, and unfortunately, that's often the case. The situation is complicated by the fact that many states have no uniform licensing requirements. Everyone has heard tales of shoddy workmanship and irresponsible behavior. There are also stories about contractors taking money for a job, starting the work and disappearing before the job is done. It's precisely these issues of lack of quality and responsibility (financial and otherwise) that form the basis of homeowners' skepticism and mistrust when it comes to the contracting industry. Be assured that there are many reputable contractors in the industry - you just have to know how to find them.

THE BIDDING PROCESS

The key to finding a reputable contractor is to recognize that a contractor's price is no indication of the quality of his work or whether he will finish the job. Obviously you want to get a good price for the work, but finding a reputable contractor should be your first concern. If you choose a contractor by price alone, you have no one to blame but yourself if things go awry. It's quite tempting to take the lowest bid price in order to save money; however, a bid that is substantially lower than the others is often the first indication of trouble. There are contractors who will purposely underbid a project, expecting to make money through change orders once they have the job. (A change order is any change from the agreed upon plans and specs that is initiated by the homeowner and results in a cost change to the job.) Unless you've crossed every "i" and dotted every "t", these contractors will find reason to charge you extra for items you thought were included in their price. Since most remodeling jobs involve some changes once work has begun, understanding how a contractor handles change orders is as significant as understanding his proposal. It's advantageous and revealing to discuss this matter early in the process. Remember the adage: "If it sounds too good to be true, it probably is." (A lot of people would probably add: "You get what you pay for".)

The process of bidding, then, involves more than collecting and comparing prices. It is your opportunity to meet, assess and investigate a variety of contractors before making a final selection.

The bidding process also allows you to maintain control over pricing and make informed budget decisions. Often, homeowners are so fearful of choosing the "wrong" contractor that they rely entirely on a single recommendation from a friend or family member. They won't even explore the possibility of using someone else. There are actually many good, reputable contractors out there, and it's to your benefit to make an effort to find them. If you hand your project to a single contractor without testing his or her price against others, you relinquish budget control. You'd be surprised at how much money you can save by taking advantage of the opportunity to compare estimates, review each line item and negotiate with your contractor of choice.

INTERVIEW CONTRACTORS

Get at least three contractors to bid your job but no more than five, even if you're planning a large project. Any more than five tends to make the bid review and comparison process confusing. You will probably have to contact double the number of contractors in order to get the number of bids you want. At this point in the process, most people have acquired the names of a few "good contractors" as a result of referrals from family, friends or neighbors. Continue your search by asking your real estate agent, attorney, building suppliers or vendors until you have a long enough list of contractors to call.

Call each contractor on your list and describe your job and desired time frame. Ask if the contractor would like to bid your project. Set up a time for each interested contractor to come to your home to find out what the job entails and request that he bring pictures of some of his projects to the meeting. This is your chance to develop an initial impression of him as well as your opportunity to discuss your general plans.

STEP 4

At your initial meeting:

- Make note if the contractor arrives on time.
- Ask yourself: "Is he neat and organized? Would I enjoy having him in my home?"
- Don't spend the entire time doing all the talking.
- Listen carefully to how he discusses other projects he's completed and how he presents his thoughts about your project.
- Find out about the number and types of jobs he currently has underway, how long he has been in business, and whether he is licensed and insured. (If a contractor is involved in too many projects, he may not be able to give you the attention you deserve or your project may get postponed. Your best choice is to find someone whose other jobs are similar in size to yours.)

A Word About Insurance

All legitimate contractors carry both general liability insurance and workman's compensation. The contractor's general liability policy protects your family, your home and adjacent home(s) from any damage or accidents that might occur during construction. The workman's comp. policy protects you from being liable in the event a workman gets hurt on your job. It is essential that the contractor you select carries the appropriate insurance. Having proper insurance not only protects you from liability, but it also indicates, since insurance is expensive to maintain, that the contractor is financially stable. If the contractor doesn't have the required insurance, there's no point in going any further with the discussion. Later in the process, when you're ready to sign a contract, you should insist that a copy of the contractor's insurance policies be sent to you directly from his insurance company, naming you as an additional insured. At that time, you will want to read these certificates carefully and make sure the name of the insured is, in fact, your contractor. You will also want to check out the policy limits to assure yourself that the coverage is adequate.

Give Out Your Bid Package

If you are comfortable with a contractor during your initial meeting, show him your plans and specs and get into a more detailed discussion of your project. For now, your goal is to give all the contractors you like, and only the contractors you like, a complete bid package at the end of this meeting. Let these "preferred" contractors know that you are in the process of getting competitive bids and will be evaluating all the bids at one time.

Remember to ask them to fill out and return your bid sheet even if they use their own format to prepare their estimate. Set a deadline for receiving all bids, and tell them when you will get back to them with a response. Contractors who are interested in your job will be able to prepare their bids within two weeks. Give yourself at least two weeks to study the bids once they've arrived. It's also a good idea to ask the contractors to guarantee their bids for 30 days to give you time to collect enough bids for review and comparison.

If you've changed your mind on any item included in your specs or changed the scope of work, make sure every contractor bidding your job has complete information regarding these changes.

Note: If you are not comfortable with a contractor at the initial meeting, tell him you will get back to him after you've completed your initial interviews and are ready to select the contractors to bid the work. There is no reason to indiscriminately hand out your bid package, and it is not at all uncommon to speak to a number of contractors before making final selections for getting bids.

WORKSHEET INSTRUCTIONS

The CONTRACTOR INTERVIEW worksheet covers the crucial issues you'll need to explore both at the initial interview and before you make a final decision. Make copies of the worksheet and use a separate one for each contractor.

The worksheet is divided into two sections: questions to ask at the initial meeting and questions to ask once you've received a contractor's bid. Until you narrow the field, there is little point spending your time doing a complete investigation and many contractors won't even want to give out certain information until they know they are seriously being considered for a job. When a contractor's estimate falls within reasonable range of your budget, you can follow up with a phone call and ask the remaining questions on the worksheet. At that point it's both appropriate and necessary to ask for vendor (credit) and client references, a copy of the contractor's contract, and to ask to visit a job site.

If you're worried about selecting the right contractor, take comfort that you're not alone. This is the point when most homeowners start to feel some anxiety. They recognize that choosing a good contractor for the "team" is critical to the success of their project. By knowing what questions to ask and taking the time to thoroughly investigate a contractor's work history and business practices, you give yourself the tools to make the right choice!

NOTES: LIST OF CONTRACTORS

Contractor Name	Phone Number	Appointment Date

CONTRACTOR INTERVIEW WORKSHEET

NAME _____

COMPANY NAME _____   Phone: _____

ADDRESS: _____   Mobile: _____

_____   Fax: _____

Questions to ask at your first meeting:

1. How long have you been in business? _____

2. Are you licensed? _____ For how long? _____ License # _____

3. What insurance do you carry? _____

4. What types of projects are you currently doing? _____

5. How many jobs are you doing right now? _____

6. How does my job fit into your schedule? _____

7. Who will be supervising my job? _____

8. What warranties do you provide? _____

9. How do you handle changes once the job begins? _____

After receiving bids:

1. Please provide 5 CUSTOMER REFERENCES.

Name: _____   Phone: _____

Name: _____   Phone: _____

Name: _____   Phone: _____

Name: _____   Phone: _____

Name: _____   Phone: _____

STEP 4

2. May I have 3 TRADE/CREDIT references?

Name: _____ Phone: _____

Name: _____ Phone: _____

Name: _____ Phone: _____

3. May I visit one of your job sites? _____

4. When could you start? _____

5. How much time will it take to complete my project? _____

6. Can you provide me with a sample contract? _____

CLIENT & CREDIT REFERENCES

When you receive the bids, phone the references for the contractors with whom you think you might like to work. Don't skip this step! Regardless of any positive impression you may have, it's necessary to investigate both credit and client references to determine a contractor's financial stability and reputation and hear how he follows through on his initial promises. Customer references will address the quality of the contractor's work; vendor/credit references will attest to financial stability.

Check References!

Check References!

Check References!

Call your Better Business Bureau (or the equivalent group in your community) and your State Licensing Bureau to confirm that each contractor does have a license and that they do not have a large number of complaints on file. It's not unusual for a contractor who has been in business for a while to have a couple of dissatisfied clients. Most contractors have had some problems or delays on their jobs, so you'll need to keep an open mind to decide whether the complaints were justified or not. Too many complaints, however, indicate trouble.

WORKSHEET INSTRUCTIONS

The CONTRACTOR REFERENCES worksheet is designed to help you get a sense of a contractor's reputation and work habits. Create a separate sheet for each customer you call. Because you will be speaking with a variety of references - individual personalities with different expectations and perceptions - be fair to yourself and the contractor by not relying on one person's opinion. In fact, if you hear some negative opinions about a contractor you particularly like, ask the contractor for an explanation.

First call the customer references listed on your Contractor Interview worksheet. Take the time to get a full impression about what it was like to work with each contractor. If you are satisfied with this information, call the vendor/credit references. All you need to ask these credit references are two simple questions:

1) Does this contractor pay his bills on time?
2) Has there ever been a history of payment problems with this contractor?

When you've finished your calls, attach the reference sheets to the appropriate Contractor Interview worksheets. Together they will give you a good overall picture of each contractor and how he operates.

It's foolish to choose a contractor by bid price alone. It's only after you've interviewed contractors and checked their reputations that you can begin to compare the prices of the contractors who remain on your list.

STEP 4

NOTES: VENDOR/CREDIT COMMENTS

_____

_____

_____

_____

_____

_____

_____

_____

_____

_____

_____

_____

_____

CONTRACTOR'S REFERENCES WORKSHEET

Contractor Name: _____

Customer Name: _____ Phone: _____

Project Description: _____

1. Was it easy to work with this contractor? _____

2. Were you happy with the quality of the work? _____

3. Was your job done on schedule? _____

4. Was (s)he responsive to your concerns? _____

5. Did (s)he perform a daily clean-up? _____

6. Was the job kept orderly and neat? _____

7. Was the contractor good at problem solving? _____

8. Were you pleased with his/her subcontractors' work? _____

9. Did this contractor supply daily on-site supervision? _____

10. Were there many change orders? _____

11. Did the contractor return to complete final details? _____

12. Would you use him/her again? _____

13. What did you like about him/her? _____

14. Did you have particular dislikes about him/her? _____

_____

_____

_____

_____

_____

CHECKLIST FOR THE BIDDING PROCESS

If you are looking for contractors to bid your project:

- ❏ Have you checked with your local lumber yard or building supply store?
- ❏ Did you ask realtors? Attorneys? Architects?
- ❏ Do you know who remodeled the homes you liked?
- ❏ Did you narrow your prospective bidders' list to five contractors?

When you are selecting the contractors to bid:

- ❏ Did this contractor return your call promptly?
- ❏ Is this contractor interested in your project?
- ❏ Can you communicate with this contractor?
- ❏ Did this contractor listen to you during your interview?
- ❏ Does this contractor have the experience for your job?
- ❏ Does this contractor seem creative?
- ❏ Does this contractor have the required insurance?
- ❏ Would you be comfortable having this contractor in your home?

When you hand out your bid package:

- ❏ Did you review your plans and specs with every contractor bidding your job?
- ❏ Does every contractor have the same specs?
- ❏ Does every contractor have the same drawings?
- ❏ Did you give a Bid Sheet to every contractor and specifically ask that it be filled out and returned?
- ❏ If you made any changes since preparing your bid package, did you notify all contractors?
- ❏ Did you set a deadline date for bids to be returned?
- ❏ Are all bids good for 30 days?

STEP 4

STEP 4

Evaluate & Compare The Bids

Deadline day - the day bids are due - has arrived! Take yourself, your worksheets, a calculator and a few sharp pencils to a quiet place so you can review the bids carefully. If your drawings and specs are clear and consistent, the legitimate bids should fall within close range of each other.

WHY BIDS VARY

A contractor determines the price he'll charge for a project by adding up his costs for labor, materials, overhead and profit. While there are variations in overhead costs and profit percentages, the cost of purchasing materials and paying prevailing labor rates is basically the same for all contractors.

Bids that are substantially out of range of the others - 20% higher *or* lower than other bids - result from one or more of the following:

1. lack of detail in your specifications causing variations in the materials being priced
2. differences in contractor overhead costs
3. variables in the profit margins contractors build into projects
4. mistakes in determining quantities or errors in arithmetic
5. a misunderstanding of part of your project
6. a lack of desire or time to work on your project
7. a willingness by the contractor to bid whatever it takes to win your job
8. a plan to increase the project costs with change orders once the work begins

Now you can see why it's so important to fully investigate a contractor's reputation before reviewing his bid. An honest and responsible contractor might make an error while compiling his bid price, but reviewing his bid will probably reveal that he falls in line price-

Your goal is to find the best contractor for your job at the best possible price.

wise on most project categories. Your task, as you compare all the bids, is to determine what's fair and reasonable for the work you want done.

HOW TO REVIEW A BID

When reviewing estimates, the first thing to do is to compare each bid to your plans and specs to make sure everything in your workplan has been included. Before you can compare prices, you must understand exactly what each contractor has included in his bid.

WORKSHEET INSTRUCTIONS

The BID REVIEW worksheet will help you organize bid information and make it easier for you to review each bid. There are three worksheets provided. If you have received more than three bids, create an additional sheet for each contractor so you have a separate sheet for each bid. Then assign each contractor a number.

Take your time as you fill in this worksheet.

- Transfer the Workplan items from your Specifications worksheet into the column marked "Workplan Item & Detail".
- Go through each bid separately, item by item, to see if all items in your specs have been quoted. If so, mark "yes" in the appropriate column.
- Check to see if the type and quality of any materials and products are the same or different than those you specified.
- If an item has been substituted, changed or omitted, circle "no" and then note the specific product that has been quoted.

Individual Bid Review Worksheet

Contractor #1: _____ **Start date:** _____

Project duration: _____

WORKPLAN ITEM & DETAIL	**INCLUDED IN BID**

1. _____ YES ____ NO _____

2. _____ YES ____ NO _____

3. _____ YES ____ NO _____

4. _____ YES ____ NO _____

5. _____ YES ____ NO _____

6. _____ YES ____ NO _____

7. _____ YES ____ NO _____

8. _____ YES ____ NO _____

9. _____ YES ____ NO _____

10. _____ YES ____ NO _____

11. _____ YES ____ NO _____

12. _____ YES ____ NO _____

13. _____ YES ____ NO _____

14. _____ YES ____ NO _____

15. _____ YES ____ NO _____

16. _____ YES ____ NO _____

17. _____ YES ____ NO _____

STEP 5

WORKPLAN ITEM & DETAIL	INCLUDED IN BID

18. _____ YES ____ NO _____

19. _____ YES ____ NO _____

20. _____ YES ____ NO _____

21. _____ YES ____ NO _____

22. _____ YES ____ NO _____

23. _____ YES ____ NO _____

24. _____ YES ____ NO _____

25. _____ YES ____ NO _____

Questions about this bid:

_____

_____

_____

_____

_____

_____

_____

_____

_____

STEP 5

Individual Bid Review Worksheet

Contractor #2: _____ **Start date:** _____

Project duration: _____

WORKPLAN ITEM & DETAIL	**INCLUDED IN BID**

1. _____ YES ___ NO _____

2. _____ YES ___ NO _____

3. _____ YES ___ NO _____

4. _____ YES ___ NO _____

5. _____ YES ___ NO _____

6. _____ YES ___ NO _____

7. _____ YES ___ NO _____

8. _____ YES ___ NO _____

9. _____ YES ___ NO _____

10. _____ YES ___ NO _____

11. _____ YES ___ NO _____

12. _____ YES ___ NO _____

13. _____ YES ___ NO _____

14. _____ YES ___ NO _____

15. _____ YES ___ NO _____

16. _____ YES ___ NO _____

17. _____ YES ___ NO _____

STEP 5

WORKPLAN ITEM & DETAIL	INCLUDED IN BID

18. _____ YES ___ NO _____

19. _____ YES ___ NO _____

20. _____ YES ___ NO _____

21. _____ YES ___ NO _____

22. _____ YES ___ NO _____

23. _____ YES ___ NO _____

24. _____ YES ___ NO _____

25. _____ YES ___ NO _____

Questions about this bid:

_____

_____

_____

_____

_____

_____

_____

_____

STEP 5

◀ INDIVIDUAL BID REVIEW WORKSHEET ────────

Contractor #3: _____ **Start date:** _____

Project duration: _____

WORKPLAN ITEM & DETAIL   INCLUDED IN BID

1. _____ YES ___ NO _____
2. _____ YES ___ NO _____
3. _____ YES ___ NO _____
4. _____ YES ___ NO _____
5. _____ YES ___ NO _____
6. _____ YES ___ NO _____
7. _____ YES ___ NO _____
8. _____ YES ___ NO _____
9. _____ YES ___ NO _____
10. _____ YES ___ NO _____
11. _____ YES ___ NO _____
12. _____ YES ___ NO _____
13. _____ YES ___ NO _____
14. _____ YES ___ NO _____
15. _____ YES ___ NO _____
16. _____ YES ___ NO _____
17. _____ YES ___ NO _____

STEP 5

WORKPLAN ITEM & DETAIL	INCLUDED IN BID

18. _____ YES ___ NO _____

19. _____ YES ___ NO _____

20. _____ YES ___ NO _____

21. _____ YES ___ NO _____

22. _____ YES ___ NO _____

23. _____ YES ___ NO _____

24. _____ YES ___ NO _____

25. _____ YES ___ NO _____

Questions about this bid:

_____

_____

_____

_____

_____

_____

_____

_____

STEP 5

Make Sure You Have Checked The Following:

❏ Does the bid include all the items in your specifications?
❏ Did you mark those items that differed from your specs?
❏ Did you review each bid carefully?
❏ Do you understand each bid?
❏ Are there areas of concern to discuss with an individual contractor?

Comparing Bids

Once you've completed the individual Bid Review worksheets, and understand what is included in each bid, you can begin your comparison of the bids.

 ## Worksheet Instructions

The BID COMPARISON worksheet helps you evaluate each contractor's price for the different categories of your project. To set up this worksheet:

■ Use the same categories you used on the Bid Sheet you gave each contractor. (Refer to Step 3)
■ The Bid # columns should correspond to the number you assigned each of the contractors. (Bid #1 was received from contractor #1.)
■ Take each contractor's Bid Sheet and transfer the category costs he outlined into the appropriate column for that contractor.

If you have more than three bids to review, make an additional Bid Comparison worksheet so that each contractor's bid can be looked at separately.

Once you've filled in all the columns, review the categories to determine the differences between bids. You can figure a reasonable cost for each category based on the dollar amounts submitted by the contractors. Here's how:

- Calculate the average category price.
- Circle those prices not in line with the other bids.
- Re-check the Specifications worksheet you put together for the contractors to see if price differences are due to differences in materials or changes made to your specs.
- Discuss any wide variances in cost with the contractor in question to discover why and how he arrived at the price.

Check to see when each contractor can start and how long each estimates the job will take. Compare the overall completeness of the bids, any written contracts submitted and payment schedules.

If something in your specifications or drawings was unclear, or if a contractor made a mistake in his calculations, you will discover it at this point. If your specs are clear, and the contractors are bidding the same work, you will see a consistency in the costs for the various categories.

NOTES: DIFFERENCES IN BID PRICES

_____

_____

_____

_____

_____

_____

_____

_____

_____

_____

BID COMPARISON WORKSHEET

	BID #1	BID #2	BID #3
1. Demolition/Debris Removal	_____	_____	_____
2. Excavation	_____	_____	_____
3. Concrete & Masonry	_____	_____	_____
4. Framing	_____	_____	_____
5. Lumber	_____	_____	_____
6. Windows & Doors	_____	_____	_____
7. Siding	_____	_____	_____
8. Roofing	_____	_____	_____
9. Gutters	_____	_____	_____
10. Landscaping	_____	_____	_____
11. Insulation	_____	_____	_____
12. Plumbing	_____	_____	_____
13. Heating	_____	_____	_____
14. Electric	_____	_____	_____
15. Drywall	_____	_____	_____
16. Finish Carpentry	_____	_____	_____
17. Painting	_____	_____	_____
18. Cabinets & Counter Tops	_____	_____	_____
19. Plumbing Fixtures	_____	_____	_____
20. Lighting Fixtures	_____	_____	_____

STEP 5

	BID #1	BID #2	BID #3
21. Flooring	_____	_____	_____
22. Ceramic Tile	_____	_____	_____
23. Hardware	_____	_____	_____
24. Miscellaneous Conditions	_____	_____	_____
25. Specialty Items	_____	_____	_____
TOTAL BID $	_____	_____	_____

STEP 5

OPTIONS FOR REDUCING COSTS

What can you do if your bids come in over budget? Actually, you have a number of choices other than throwing up your hands in despair and abandoning your project. There are four options to consider: re-select some of your materials, negotiate prices with your contractor, do some of the work yourself, or take another look at your budget and priorities.

RE-SELECT MATERIALS

Consider changing some of your material and product selections. The range of quality products (and prices!) available in the marketplace is large. Just as the most expensive item isn't always the best, inexpensive items do not always imply poor quality. Reconsider some of your selections and see if you can find acceptable substitutes. Manufacturers often offer different grades of materials within their product lines, starting with "builder's grade" and working up to the most expensive "premium grade". Check sizes of windows, doors, cabinets and vanities to make sure they are standard size, rather than custom. The difference in measurement between a standard item and a custom one might be small, but the price difference can be considerable. Also search for copies of brand name products that look the same as their more expensive counterparts yet function just as well. Once these products are installed, no one - not even you - will know the difference. It might take a little more legwork but you will find substitutes. Don't give up quality, just cut the price tag.

NEGOTIATE PRICES

Negotiate some of the line items if the estimates are just too tight for comfort. Use the Bid Comparison worksheet to evaluate the individual category costs that make up a total bid. This information allows you to negotiate the fairest price for the work to be done. If you are happy with a contractor's total bid, but one specific item is out of line with the other bids, talk to the contractor and find out how he justified the higher price. As you negotiate, keep in mind that you want to create a "win-win" situation where everyone is eager to begin the work. You don't want to negotiate quality or enthusiasm out of your job.

Do Some of The Work Yourself

Sometimes you can lower project costs by doing some of the work yourself. Some contractors will allow you to supply the labor for parts of your job, while others will not. There are pros and cons to this approach, so consider it carefully before assuming responsibility for part of the construction. Not only do contractors work within their own time schedules, but they also follow a completion schedule dictated by building departments via building permits. In order to get a final inspection and sign-off for your project from local officials, certain work must be completed. When an owner provides some of the labor for a project, the contractor no longer has control over the timing of the work. When the job you'd like to do interferes with the contractor's time schedule and work flow, there can be unpleasant consequences. Typically, they include lots of headaches for the contractor and the potential for increased costs for you.

A perfect example of this is painting. Homeowners often think the way to save money on their project is to do the painting themselves. However, they often underestimate the time it takes to complete this work. In the meantime, the contractor cannot schedule final electric work or flooring until the painting is finished. This could mean rescheduling subcontractors or finding new ones, delaying project completion and possibly escalating costs. If you would like to cut costs by contributing your labor, the best approach is to find the things you can do yourself before the contractor starts or after he has finished his work.

Review Your Budget And Priorities

If the estimates come in way beyond your expectations, analyze your budget to see if it is realistic for the work you'd like done. Assess whether to adjust the scope of work. If you are building an addition, perhaps you can amend the size. Prices for new construction typically range from $60/sq ft. on up. By changing your space requirements, you may be able to bring your costs in line. Also review your Priorities worksheet. Is there anything you can postpone without compromising the project? If necessary, create an amended set of specs and send your project out to bid again.

Meet With Your Chosen Contractor

If you think you've found the right combination of contractor and price, set up a meeting with the contractor you've selected. At this meeting, discuss any changes you would like made to your plans, bring up areas of negotiation and ask any questions you still have. Make sure your questions about guarantees, change orders, work schedules and ordering times are answered before agreeing to a contract.

CHECKLIST FOR SELECTING A CONTRACTOR

- ❑ Did you call all customer and credit references?
- ❑ Did you review the estimate to make sure you understood everything clearly?
- ❑ Did you discuss areas of negotiation?
- ❑ Did you go over the contractor's change order policy?
- ❑ Did you discuss allowances?
- ❑ Did you discuss start date and payment schedules?
- ❑ Did you discuss scheduling?
- ❑ Does this contractor guarantee his work?
- ❑ Is everything promised in writing?
- ❑ Did you visit a job site?

STEP 5

Protect Yourself With A Solid Contract

Remodeling your home is not an area where you want to do business on a handshake. Given the money you are about to spend, you want to control and protect your investment by writing a clear, detailed contract.

A good contract defines your legal relationship with the contractor, his workers and subcontractors and clearly delineates the responsibilities of all parties involved. It also details what is (and is not) included for the price you have negotiated. The contract establishes the terms of your agreement, including when the work will be done, how the contractor will get paid, and terms of recourse if something goes wrong. This single document ties together all your drawings, specifications, change orders, schedules and payment agreements. The contract needs to provide equal protection for the two main parties and must be fair to all parties involved.

You can choose from many different building and remodeling contract formats. Your contractor probably will want to use his "standard" agreement. There is, however, no such thing, and you have the right to insist on using the contract format that makes you comfortable.

Both The American Institute of Architects (AIA) and the Association of General Contractors (AGC) have good building contracts that you may be able to find in your library or by calling their local offices. You might also want to consult with your attorney who may already have a contract designed for your situation. The sample contract presented in this chapter draws from various contracts and incorporates the essential elements to be included when you create your contract documents.

Types of Agreements

There are three major approaches that set the foundation for your contract: stipulated sum, cost plus, and management.

The "Stipulated Sum" approach is really the best for homeowners, because it offers the most protection. Using this approach, you pay a fixed price for the specified work, and any changes require written change orders. The price is determined in advance, and the responsibility for doing the work for the stated sum rests entirely with the contractor.

"Cost Plus" is another approach offered by contractors to homeowners. With this agreement, you pay the invoice cost for labor and materials plus an agreed upon percentage for the contractor's overhead and profit. For the homeowner, the major problem with this approach is that the total price is in question until the very end. Contractors often offer this type of agreement as a compromise when a job is complicated by a number of unknown factors. The homeowner agrees to pay whatever the job costs as it progresses, which allows the contractor to avoid having to bid high to protect himself from hidden "surprises". Many homeowners think they can save money by going this route, but job costs can easily get out of hand. Unless you tag along with your contractor each time he purchases materials, and stay home watching the clock while he's working, you really have no idea how realistic his invoices are. In addition, the contractor has no incentive to save you money. No matter what the material and labor cost, he will get paid.

The same holds true with a "Management" approach. In this type of arrangement, the contractor accepts a set fee for his time and energy instead of a percentage of construction costs for overhead and profit. The homeowner pays invoice costs plus the contractor's fee. The benefit of this approach for the contractor is that no matter what the job costs, he makes a guaranteed amount of money based on the initial scope and projected cost of the project. If the scope of the job gets larger and additional work is required, the contractor's fee increases. Again, the contractor has no incentive to keep costs in check or to work towards cost-effective solutions.

Unless you have complete knowledge and faith that your contractor is trustworthy, it's best to avoid both the "Cost Plus" and "Management" approaches. Contracts based on either of these approaches leave too much control in the hands of the contractor. Neither approach provides you with any assurances you will be able to keep a handle on your project's final cost.

CONTRACT BASICS

No matter which contract format or payment approach you use, there are specific details that must be included in every contract in order for you to be properly protected: scope of work, project timetable, agreed price, payment schedule and lien waivers. Each is explained below.

DESCRIPTION OF WORK

Scope of Work - is a description of the work to be done. This section details the work that is and is not included in the contract and identifies who will be doing the work. You need to list who is responsible for providing any surveys, permits (both zoning and building) and inspections. While it's very common for the homeowner to supply any surveys and zoning permits required, it's best to let the contractor be responsible for obtaining the building permit. Whoever gets that permit is legally responsible for ensuring all building codes are met.

If you already addressed these matters in your specifications, you do not need to repeat this information. In fact, how much detail you spell out in the contract, in terms of the work to be done, depends on what is in your complete package of contract documents. If all this information is detailed in your specs, you can simply attach your drawings and specs to the contract. If you have any additional drawings or amendments to the specifications, be sure to note them in this section and attach them to the contract as well.

IMPORTANT DATES

Time of Completion - defines the tentative start date for your project and the estimated date of substantial completion. Ask your contractor to provide a construction timeline and include this schedule as one of your contract documents. Taking this action holds the contractor accountable for diligently pursuing his work once the job begins and gives you an indication of how the job should proceed. Unforeseen circumstances happen on every job and cause delays. A supplier may promise delivery of certain materials for one date, only to call and postpone delivery for a few days or more. The weather might make it impossible to install your roof or complete the framing of your addition. While annoying, these types of delays are inevitable and acceptable on a construction job. What you are guarding against in this section of the contract are two potential problems: failure on the contractor's part to work steadily on your job, and failure on your part to make selections and decisions in a timely fashion. When you fail to work in tandem with a contractor's schedule, you cause holdups on the job that cost the contractor money. By clarifying the project's timeline, both you and the contractor are acknowledging your mutual responsibilities.

CONTRACT PRICE AND CHANGE ORDERS

Contract Price - says, in words and number, the price you have agreed to pay for the work specified. If you are following the "Stipulated Sum" approach, this section should also state that any changes in price caused by changes in scope of work must be detailed in a written change order signed by both you and your contractor before the work is done. A change order results from your request to make changes to the agreed upon scope of work. You have a lot of control over change orders. With written change orders, you know in advance what any changes will cost and can decide whether or not to execute these changes. By insisting on written change orders, your contract price cannot change without your approval - there will be no surprises when it comes time to pay the final bill.

A change order is not the same as a cost overrun. The latter is caused by an unanticipated problem arising during the course of the job. Cost overruns are paid by the homeowner when the condition requiring additional work was unknown at the time the job was bid. However, if a contractor attempts to charge you for something he forgot to include in his bid, as long as you have a "stipulated sum" agreement, it is his cost to bear. As you progress through the construction process, you will need to fairly evaluate whether something is truly a cost overrun or the result of a contractor's error at the time he bid your job.

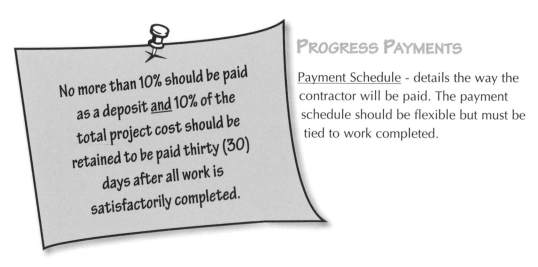

No more than 10% should be paid as a deposit <u>and</u> 10% of the total project cost should be retained to be paid thirty (30) days after all work is satisfactorily completed.

PROGRESS PAYMENTS

Payment Schedule - details the way the contractor will be paid. The payment schedule should be flexible but must be tied to work completed.

PROGRESS PAYMENT PERCENTAGES	FOR $10,000 JOB
Downpayment - no more than 10%	$ 1,000
Drywall complete	$ 2,700
Cabinets & counters installed	$ 2,700
Completion	$ 2,600
Retainage - 10%	$ 1,000

Note: The only exception to a 10% deposit would be when a supplier requires a larger deposit before ordering specific materials. For example, kitchen and bath showrooms often require a 50% deposit at time of order. However, you would pay such deposits directly to the supplier, not to the contractor.

Payments should be evenly spread out and correspond to specific milestones of completed work. Obviously, your own payment schedule will depend on the work you have specified, but do not issue payment until major portions of your job have been completed!

Holding 10% retainage for thirty (30) days, gives you a chance to make sure all the work has been done satisfactorily and allows the contractor time to respond to your final checklists.

If you have a large project, your payment schedule is likely to be more complicated than the $10,000 project example. You can calculate a reasonable payment schedule by using your Bid Sheet:

- Go through each bid item to determine its percentage of total contract cost.
- Calculate the amount to be paid at the completion of each category.
- Take 10% of each category's cost as your deposit amount.
- Hold 10% of each category's cost as retainage.

There is an alternative to progress payments. You may request that the contractor give you a payment and performance "bond" or "contract of indemnity", which guarantees that your money will be properly used or returned. However, most small contractors are not likely to have the financial resources needed to obtain a bond and typically prefer the progress payment arrangement.

STEP 6

Lien Waivers

Your contract must call for the contractor to provide signed and notarized lien waivers for each payment he and his subcontractors receive. A lien waiver is your proof that a worker has been paid. Any contractor, subcontractor and/or supplier who has performed work or supplied material to your job is entitled to file a mechanic's lien on your property if they are not paid. Once paid, the right to file a lien is waived. If you've paid your contractor but he does not pay his subcontractors, you are held financially responsible for their payment. To protect yourself from any fiduciary negligence on the part of your contractor, insist on lien waivers from all who work on your job. Collecting lien waivers with every progress payment allows you to monitor whether or not all workers on your job are being paid.

Sample Contract

Following are the initial pages of a sample contract, showing you how these sections are presented in an actual contract document.

This sample contract is provided as a guide. Consider it carefully as no standard form can meet all requirements. It is believed to be reliable but is not guaranteed.

STEP 6

BUILDING & REMODELING CONTRACT

Contract made this _____ day of _____ , ___ (year), between _____
hereinafter referred to as OWNER residing at _____ and
_____ , hereinafter
referred to as CONTRACTOR, with offices at _____
_____ .

   The parties to this Agreement, in consideration of the mutual covenants and stipulations set out, agree to the Scope of Work as set forth in the Contract plans and specifications, all written addenda mutually agreed upon and issued prior to the execution of this Agreement, and all written modifications mutually issued by the Owner and Contractor after execution of the Contract including Change Orders. These form the Contract Documents and are fully part of the Contract.

SECTION I

CONTRACT AS ENTIRE AGREEMENT

   This Contract contains the entire agreement between the parties, and no statements, promises, or inducements made by either party or agent of either party that are not contained in this contract shall be valid or binding; this Contract may not be enlarged, modified or altered except in writing signed by both parties and endorsed on this Agreement.

SECTION II

AGREEMENT

ARTICLE 1. SCOPE OF THE WORK

   The Contractor shall furnish all of the materials and perform all of the Work as described in the Contract Documents as it pertains to the work to be performed on the property at:
_____ .

STEP 6

ARTICLE 2.   TIME OF COMPLETION

2.1   The work to be performed under this Contract shall be commenced on or before _____ , and shall be substantially completed on or before _____ .

2.2   Owner will furnish to Contractor, prior to commencement of the Work, reasonable evidence of financial ability to fulfill the Owner's obligation under this Contract.

2.3   Contractor agrees to start and diligently pursue the Work through completion. However, Substantial Completion may be extended because of delays beyond the Contractor's control, including but not limited to: Delays in issuance of necessary building permits, adverse weather conditions, availability of materials or labor, illness, unavoidable casualties, any act or neglect of Owner, architect or designer, additional work or changes requested by Owner, failure of Owner to make payments when due, delays occasioned by acts of God, strikes, changes in governmental regulations, catastrophes, wars, riots and all similar occurrences beyond Contractor's, his subcontractors' or suppliers' control.

2.4   Owner agrees that the date of Substantial Completion may be extended for a reasonable period of time without incurring damages or penalty for such delays.

2.5   Substantial Completion is that date when the Work is sufficiently completed as to obtain any final inspections stipulated by the building permit or when the OWNER can occupy, utilize or continue the Work in conjunction with the use for which it was intended, whichever occurs first.

ARTICLE 3.   THE CONTRACT PRICE

3.1   The Owner shall pay the Contractor for the performance of the Work under the Contract the sum of _____ Dollars ($ _____), subject to additions and deductions pursuant to authorized Change Orders.

3.2   Upon reasonable request by Owner, the Contractor will make alterations, additions or substitutions to the Work and Contract price, and Substantial Completion will be modified accordingly, as set out in a written Change Order. All Change Orders shall be in writing and signed by both Owner and Contractor, and shall be incorporated in and become part of the Contract.

3.3   Any adjustment in the Contract price resulting in a credit or a charge to the Owner will be determined by mutual consent of the parties, before starting the work involved in the change. In some cases a deposit will be required before starting the work and, in all cases, changes will be paid in full upon completion of the change order work.

3.4   Owner agrees to make requests concerning any changes, additions or substitutions directly to the Contractor and not to his workers or subcontractors on the worksite.

3.5   If the Contract price and specifications include allowances, and the cost is greater or less than the allowance figure included, the Contract price will be adjusted accordingly.

ARTICLE 4.   PROGRESS PAYMENTS

4.1   Based upon applications for payment submitted to the Owner by the Contractor, the Owner shall make progress payments on account of the Contract Sum to the Contractor as follows: All payments shall be due on the day indicated.

_____

_____

_____

_____

_____

_____

_____

4.2   Any monies not paid in accordance with the Contract Documents shall bear interest from the date payment is due at 1% per month.

4.3   Payments may be withheld without interest, from Contractor by Owner, in an amount equal to the Work in question, due to significantly defective Work not remedied or persistent failure by Contractor to carry out the work in accordance with the Contract Documents.

4.4   Final payment, constituting the entire unpaid balance of the Contract Sum, shall be paid by the Owner to the Contractor no more than 30 days after the Work is entirely complete.

4.5   The Contractor will furnish the Owner appropriate releases or lien waivers for all work performed or materials provided at the time the next periodic payment shall be due. Final payment will not be due until Contractor delivers to Owner a complete release of all liens arising out of this agreement. If any lien remains unsatisfied after all payments are made, Contractor will refund to Owner all monies paid by Owner to discharge such lien, including all cost and reasonable attorney's fees.

THE REMAINDER OF THE CONTRACT

The balance of the contract contains a section addressing miscellaneous conditions affecting the job, as well as a section dealing with termination and default.

GENERAL PROVISIONS

General Provisions - As the name implies, this section contains a variety of statements related to conduct on the job, warranties, insurance and dispute settlement. You can also include requirements for clean-up, penalties or any special situations you want to apply to your project. This is the contract section that is most flexible and really is the place to lay out all the miscellaneous terms of your agreement with your contractor. Read this section in the sample contract carefully to see all the different conditions that it covers.

One of the biggest problems that occurs on a project involving more than one workman is when a homeowner circumvents the contractor and asks an employee or subcontractor to do "extra" work or make some adjustment to the established workplan. Homeowners don't recognize that employees and subcontractors don't always know the full extent of the project. In order for a remodeling job to run smoothly, the contractor in charge must be informed of all work being done or any changes to be made. It really is in your best interest to know who is in charge of your project and to discuss all changes only with him.

Warranties - There should be a statement included in your contract holding your contractor responsible for his work for a period of at least one year. If your contractor has any written statement of warranty, attach it to your contract as an addendum. The warranty your contractor provides is your assurance that the contractor or his subcontractors will take care of anything included in the scope of work needing repair after final payment is made. Generally, a contractor's warranty is for one year from date of completion on labor and materials. There are also extended warranties offered on structural components or manufacturer's products, such as water heaters, roofing or siding materials. A full warranty means that all faulty products must be repaired or replaced or your money returned. A limited warranty means that there is some monetary restriction in regard to refunds and replacements.

Insurance - In Step 4 - Find Reputable Contractors To Bid, you learned about liability and workman's comp. insurance requirements. Your contract should call for copies of these insurance policies to be sent directly to you from the insurance companies with your name as certificate holder. No work should be started until you are in receipt of these certificates of insurance.

Arbitration - It would be foolish for you to enter into any contract agreement without recognizing that something could go wrong and you might be unable to resolve the problem directly with your contractor. It is common to address this issue by calling for any disputes to be resolved through arbitration, a procedure that is far less expensive than going to court. You can designate an arbitration group, such as the American Arbitration Association, or any third party mutually agreed to by you and the contractor.

TERMINATION AND DEFAULT

Termination and Default - Default deals with the breach of contract by either you or your contractor and addresses the failure of either party to fulfill their contractual obligations, including work and payment agreements. A termination clause defines the rights of both owner and contractor if termination becomes necessary.

The final pages of the sample contract follow. They show how the sections involving general provisions and termination and default are organized and presented.

BUILDING & REMODELING CONTRACT
(continued)

ARTICLE 5.   GENERAL PROVISIONS

5.1   All work shall be completed in a workman-like manner and in compliance with all building codes and other applicable laws.
5.2   To the extent required by law all work shall be performed by individuals duly licensed and authorized by law to perform said work.
5.3   The Contractor may at his discretion engage subcontractors to perform work hereunder, provided the Contractor shall fully pay said subcontractors and in all instances remain responsible for the proper completion of this contract.
5.4   The Owner will have no authority to negotiate with Contractor's workers or subcontractors or to directly subcontract any of the Work described herein or to have any subcontractor work at the site under the terms of this Contract without the written approval of the Contractor.

STEP 6

5.5   The Contractor will have sole control of the construction personnel, including sub-contractors. Owner will not issue any instructions or otherwise interfere with construction personnel, including subcontractors.

5.6   The Contractor warrants he is adequately insured for injury to his employees and others incurring loss or injury as a result of the acts of the Contractor or his employees or subcontractors. Certificates of general liability and workman's compensation will be sent to Owner prior to any work beginning.

5.7   The Contractor agrees to remove all debris and leave the premises in broom clean condition.

5.8   In the event the Owner shall fail to pay any periodic or installment payment due hereunder, the Contractor may cease work without breach, pending payment or resolution of any dispute.

5.9   The Contractor warrants all work for a period of _____ months following completion.

5.10   All disputes hereunder shall be resolved by binding arbitration in accordance with the American Arbitration Association. Notwithstanding this provision, nothing will preclude Contractor's right to pursue the lien remedies and procedures as provided within the laws of _____ (your state).

5.11   If either party becomes involved in arbitration or litigation arising out of this agreement or its performance, reasonable cost and expense of arbitration and attorney's fees may be awarded to the party who recovers judgment.

5.12   Other provisions:

_____

_____

_____

_____

_____

_____

ARTICLE 6. TERMINATION AND DEFAULT.

6.1   If Owner fails to comply with the provisions of this Contract, Contractor may terminate this Contract and retain any deposit or Monies received as liquidated damages, or at the option of the Contractor, Contractor may proceed for specific performance or any other available legal or equitable remedies.

Owner will be in default under this Contract if any of the following take place:

a.   Owner fails or refuses to pay within five (5) days any amount set forth in this Agreement.

b.   Owner in any way fails or refuses to perform any provision of this Agreement required of Owner.

c. Owner makes any assignment for benefit of creditors or files any petition under any bankruptcy, insolvency or debtor relief law.

6.2 If Contractor fails to comply with the provisions of this Contract, Owner may terminate this Contract.

Contractor will be in default under this Contract if any of the following take place:

a. Contractor fails or refuses to do the Work in accordance with the Contract Documents after ten (10) days written notice from Owner.

b. Contractor makes any assignment for benefit of creditors or files any petition under any bankruptcy, insolvency or debtor relief law.

SECTION III

EFFECT OF AGREEMENT

This agreement shall inure to the benefit of and be binding on the heirs, executors, assignees and successors of the respective parties. Neither party will have the right to assign, transfer or sublet his/her interests or obligations hereunder without the written consent of the other party. If two or more parties are named herein as OWNER, their obligation will be joint and several.

IN WITNESS WHEREOF, the parties have executed this agreement on the day and year first above written.

_____   _____
OWNER'S NAME   CONTRACTOR'S NAME

_____   _____
OWNER 'S SIGNATURE   CONTRACTOR'S SIGNATURE

STEP 6

You have the legal right to cancel your contract within 3 days of signing it. To do so, you must notify your contractor in writing. Any deposits you've paid must be returned within 10 business days following the contractor's receipt of your written notice.

WORKSHEET INSTRUCTIONS

You can use the CONTRACT INFORMATION worksheet to compile the information you need to prepare your complete contract. You might also want to attach this worksheet to the front of whatever contract form you use as a summary sheet.

Make sure the contractor's business name is legally correct. His address should be the address where he keeps his legal records and not a post office box. If your state requires contractors to be licensed, make sure you have obtained the contractor's correct license number.

Calculate your payment schedule and make a list of all the individual documents you have that are to be attached to your contract as part of your agreement: drawings, specifications, contractor's proposal, change orders, timelines and list of subcontractors.

Don't be reluctant to insist on using your own choice of contract documents with your contractor. As long as you are fair and try to evaluate each issue from both perspectives, these documents will serve not only to protect you but your contractor as well.

NOTES: INCLUDE IN CONTRACT

_____

_____

_____

_____

_____

_____

_____

_____

_____

_____

STEP 6

Contract Information Worksheet

CONTRACTOR _____

COMPANY NAME _____

ADDRESS (not PO Box) _____

PHONE: _____ PAGER: _____ FAX: _____

LICENSE # (if applicable) _____

OVERALL SCOPE OF PROJECT:

_____

_____

OTHER ITEMS TO BE DONE: Include surveys, zoning and/or building permits

   BY OWNER:

_____

_____

   BY CONTRACTOR:

_____

_____

   BY ARCHITECT/ENGINEER/DESIGNER

_____

_____

START DATE _____ EST. COMPLETION DATE _____

TOTAL CONTRACT PRICE _____

PAYMENT SCHEDULE:

WORK COMPLETED   PAYMENT AMOUNT

_____   _____

_____   _____

_____   _____

_____   _____

_____   _____

_____   _____

LIST OF ADDENDUM TO ATTACH:

_____

_____

_____

_____

_____

_____

RECEIVED: YES   NO

INSURANCE CERTIFICATES   ☐   ☐

LIST OF SUBCONTRACTORS   ☐   ☐

STEP 6

DO NOT SIGN A CONTRACT OR PAY ANY MONIES AS DEPOSIT UNTIL:

❏ The contractor has provided you with a timetable for construction.

❏ You have received a list of subcontractors, if applicable.

❏ You have received the contractor's liability and workman's comp. insurance certificates.

❏ Everything promised is in writing.

STEP 6

STEP 6

Oversee The Work In Progress

You are ready for construction to start! You've cleared your personal belongings from the space to be remodeled so your contractor has a clean place to work. You've finalized all your decisions. Your contractor has given you a work schedule and list of subcontractors so you have an idea of who will be involved in the work ahead. It's a very exciting time, but it is also a time to maintain control over your project.

THE PRE-CONSTRUCTION MEETING

The very first day of the job is the time to set clear guidelines for all who will be working in your home. Regardless of your project's size, remodeling is disruptive and messy but there are measures you can take to contain the mess and minimize the invasion of your privacy. The pre-construction meeting is your opportunity to establish some ground rules for the use of your home.

- <u>Work hours</u> - Agree on a work schedule that satisfies everyone concerned. Clarify the time when workmen can arrive in the morning and their quitting time at the end of the day. Discuss whether work will be done on weekends or holidays.

- <u>The staging area</u> - Where will the contractor store materials and tools? Will he use the garage or basement, or is there some other area you can allocate? Find an area that can be accessed easily and is as close to the work area as possible.

- <u>Entrances and bathroom facilities</u> - Inform the contractor which entrance door(s) and bathroom(s) the workmen can use.

- <u>Keys and alarms</u> - Who will have a key (if anyone)? Will the contractor be expected to lock up and set the alarm when he leaves?

- <u>Clean-up</u> - Insist that your contractor do a quick clean-up at the end of every day. This not only prevents accidents, but also makes it easier for you to inspect job progress. Your clean-up requirements should also be included in your contract.

- <u>Family privacy</u> - Point out rooms that are to be off limits to workmen and ask that the workspace be divided from your living space. Heavy plastic sheeting taped over wall or door openings will provide a privacy barrier and help keep dirt away from the rest of the house.

- <u>Protection of other space</u> - Bring attention to the walls and floors that are not being redone and insist that care be taken by all workers. Ask that drop cloths be used on the floors that the workmen will be using.

As your job progresses, remind your contractor to inform all new workmen or subcontractors of these ground rules so they are maintained to your satisfaction.

THE 6 PRINCIPLES OF PROJECT MANAGEMENT

It's very easy, as work proceeds, to make some common - and often expensive - mistakes. If you adhere to six important project management principles, you'll stay on top of both your budget and your project as you move through the various stages of construction.

1. <u>Avoid Changes</u>. One of the easiest ways to go over budget, is to find additional work for your contractor to do outside your contract agreement. For example, while your kitchen is being remodeled, you remember that your bedroom closet doors need to be replaced or you'd like a window seat built in your daughter's playroom. Your contractor is easy to work with and eager to please. It doesn't seem like a large request to you, especially since the contractor is already there. When you ask him about these "minor" extras, he assures you they are no problem and probably won't cost very much, but he doesn't quote you a definite price. When you receive the bill you may be unpleasantly surprised.

The reason you spent all the time planning your project was to avoid this very situation. Tackling extras while the contractor is working in your home seems logical, but last-minute work can be more costly than if it had been included in your original plans. It's an interesting industry statistic that the average remodeling project winds up costing 20% more than originally planned because of change orders. Figure it out! If you're planning a $25,000 project, you could incur (if you aren't careful) another $5,000 because you changed your mind and found additional work to do during the course of your job. If you fall into this trap you will only be able to blame yourself when costs get out of hand!

The better plan is to wait until you review and evaluate a written change order before agreeing to any additional work. Better yet, if you find you have a reasonable number of miscellaneous extras to be done in your home, make a list and turn them into a separate project. Your contractor may be able to do this mini-project cheaper at a slower time of year or you may be able to hire a handyman for fewer dollars.

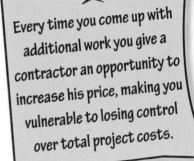

Every time you come up with additional work you give a contractor an opportunity to increase his price, making you vulnerable to losing control over total project costs.

2. <u>Be flexible</u>. Remodeling is very different than building something from scratch. You are working with existing conditions, some of them hidden, and you never really know what problems may arise until you get into construction. Be prepared to compromise. Be flexible in your approach to these surprises in order to find solutions that work for both your budget and your design. If you hold on to a design concept or an idea despite complicating conditions, you will find yourself paying a high price for your determination to execute a specific detail. Cost overruns occur when actual conditions turn out to be different than what you and your contractor expected at the time you signed your contract. Keep an open mind and look for solutions that make sense for the overall project. Step back, relax and discuss the various options and costs with your contractor before you make any decisions.

3. <u>Be available</u>. There will always be some decisions that need to be made during construction that couldn't be anticipated in advance. If you are not available to make decisions, someone else will make them for you. Problems always arise when home owners assume that everyone involved in executing the project understands what the homeowner wants. Assume nothing and make sure you have established a consistent

way to communicate with your contractor every day. If there are subcontractors on the job, have your contractor introduce you so you know who they are and what they are supposed to do. Review the work accomplished each day and question your contractor (not the subcontractors or crew) about anything that does not seem right to you. Contractors are human and do make mistakes, but it's much easier to correct mistakes when they first happen than if you wait until all the work is completed. Use your project notebook to keep a log of your daily inspections and to track questions, concerns and answers.

4. Make timely decisions. By signing your contract, you and the contractor mutually agreed to complete your respective duties in a responsible way. Just as you don't want to incur inconvenience or additional expense because of something your contractor does, the contractor doesn't want to lose time or money because of your inability to make timely decisions. The work schedule provided by your contractor should serve as your project guide, indicating when you can expect different types of work to occur. It is also your personal timetable for making decisions and ordering products. If a contractor has to stop work because materials haven't yet been ordered, or you're having difficulty coming to a decision, it will ultimately cost you time and money for these delays. Make a list of items you will need to select and find out when your selections are required in order for the job to progress smoothly. For example, kitchen cabinets can take 2-3 months to be delivered from order date. Create a schedule for making your selections that works along with your contractor's timeline and keep a copy in your notebook.

TIMELINE: IMPORTANT DATES

Products	Final date for ordering
_____	_____
_____	_____
_____	_____
_____	_____
_____	_____
_____	_____

STEP 7

5. <u>Don't be afraid to stop the job</u>. If the job doesn't get off to a good start or you are unhappy with the quality of work being done - call a halt! Trust your instincts. After all, it's your home and you will be living with the end product for many years to come. In the long run you want to be satisfied with your choices and their execution. If something has to be changed, now is the time so that you're not left with a finished product you dislike.

6. <u>Relax</u>. No matter how tight your contract, there is no substitute for a good relationship with your contractor. If you have taken all the suggested steps in preparation and planning, the work now belongs to the contractor while you stay available but out of the way. Trust your contractor (unless he proves unworthy) and let him do his work in an unencumbered fashion. Homeowners create a lot of confusion and cause costly mistakes when they interfere with a contractor's crew. It's best to establish a positive working relationship with your contractor, review the job at the end of every day and create a communication system that works. If you do these things, you'll go a long way toward ensuring the project is executed as you planned.

Keep these 6 principles firmly in mind as you monitor each phase in the construction process.

STAGES OF CONSTRUCTION

You do not need technical expertise as the work progresses, but it does help to understand the sequence of work and the order of inspections in order to prepare for any decisions you might have to make.

<u>Demolition</u> - Before the contractor can build new space or install your new fixtures, cabinets or other items, the old space must be cleared out. Have your contractor close off the area undergoing construction. Cover any heating or air conditioner units and smoke alarms and remove all personal belongings from the area. If a dumpster is required, talk to your contractor about where it should be placed on your property. If a dumpster will not be needed, find out how the contractor plans to remove debris from your home.

STEP 7

Demolition: Questions & Concerns

_____

_____

_____

_____

_____

Re-building - Depending on your project, re-building might start with a new foundation or with framing in new walls. This is where the first building permit inspections will occur. Again, depending on the scope of work, there will be permit inspections for both footings and the foundation, and an inspection of the rough framing.

Re-building: Questions & Concerns

_____

_____

_____

_____

_____

_____

Rough Mechanicals - While the walls are still open, any ductwork for heating, piping for plumbing, tubs and showers, and electrical wiring will be installed. Wiring is run for switches, outlets, phone lines and speakers, with rectangular boxes tacked into the studs to hold these items. Take time to check the placement of these boxes to make sure you are satisfied with the number and location of switches and outlets. Adding additional switches/outlets after the fact will be expensive. _In fact, this is the point after which you will not be able to add any recessed fixtures or built-ins without moving "backwards" in the construction process._ The walls will be closed in by insulation and drywall after this "roughing" is complete, so take your time to make sure everything is laid out as you want.

There will be another inspection once this work is completed to ensure all was done according to code.

ROUGH MECHANICALS: QUESTIONS & CONCERNS

_____

_____

_____

_____

_____

_____

Insulation & Drywall - These two items quickly follow each other and often are done by the same subcontractor. Installing insulation is accomplished quickly, but completing drywall is a tedious and messy task. Once the drywall is hung it needs to be taped, coated and sanded to create a smooth joint where the sheets of drywall meet. This process requires that the drywaller come back to your home a number of times. Seal off the remodeled space as much as possible in order to keep the "dust" created from sanding away from the rest of the house. Drywalling really is the messiest part of the job and once it's finished, you're on the way to seeing finished products fill the space.

INSULATION & DRYWALL: QUESTIONS & CONCERNS

_____

_____

_____

_____

_____

_____

STEP 7

Trim - Trim includes cabinets and countertops, railing systems, doors, baseboards, mantels and any specialty items that would be installed by a finish carpenter. These types of materials have the longest lag time when it comes to delivery and must be ordered well in advance of their installation date in order to arrive at your home on time.

TRIM: QUESTIONS & CONCERNS

_____

_____

_____

_____

_____

_____

Painting - It is common to apply a primer and first coat of paint to the walls along with a finish coat to the ceilings at this point in the job. A finish wall coat is applied after all your plumbing and electrical fixtures have been installed.

PAINTING: QUESTIONS & CONCERNS

_____

_____

_____

_____

_____

_____

STEP 7

Flooring - Carpeting is not installed until all the remaining work is finished, but vinyl flooring, tile and hardwood can be installed at this stage of the job.

FLOORING: QUESTIONS & CONCERNS

_____

_____

_____

_____

_____

Finish Mechanicals - This includes lighting, cover plates for switches and outlets, sinks, faucets, toilets, heating and air conditioning units. Your contractor needs to have the lighting fixtures and faucets you've selected available on the job.

FINISH MECHANICALS: QUESTIONS & CONCERNS

_____

_____

_____

_____

_____

STEP 7

Finish Painting - The final coat of paint is applied to walls and trim. It's a good idea to ask that extra paint be left on your job and clearly marked so it can be used for any touchups needed after final clean-up.

FINISH PAINTING: QUESTIONS & CONCERNS

_____

_____

_____

_____

_____

Finish Flooring - Any flooring that has not been completed is done at this time. Once the finish flooring is done, there will be inspections for the heating, plumbing and electric systems, followed by a final building inspection to ensure that your new space is safe and ready for you to use.

FINISH FLOORING: QUESTIONS & CONCERNS

_____

_____

_____

_____

_____

STEP 7

Miscellaneous - Final "clean-up" is the time when attention is paid to all the odds and ends of the job. Doors might need to be cut down to clear carpeting. Accessory items like towel bars, toilet paper holders, door and closet knobs, mirrors, etc. will be installed. Once the contractor finishes these items, he cleans up and removes both his equipment and any remaining debris from your home.

MISCELLANEOUS: QUESTIONS & CONCERNS

_____

_____

_____

_____

_____

_____

YOUR FINAL INSPECTION

Once all permit inspections are done, your project is considered to have reached the point of "substantial completion". Your remodeling is basically complete and you should be able to move in. According to your contract documents, at the time of substantial completion, your contractor is entitled to his total contract price minus a 10% retainage as hold back for small, incidental repairs. Before writing out the check, however, there is one major thing to do.

Take your time to complete a thorough inspection.

Make sure all the work is really completed.
Inspect the job by yourself when you have the time to focus on details. Usually by the time most homeowners reach this stage, they are ready for all the contractors and crew to leave so they can settle in and regain their privacy. In the excitement and haste to call the job complete, it's easy to see the big picture and miss the small details. Don't write flaws off by saying, "nothing's perfect". You have the right to expect top quality products and workmanship on every aspect of your job. The Construction Standards in the appendix are your guide to standards of quality and performance. Refer to these standards when issues of quality arise.

STEP 7

WORKSHEET INSTRUCTIONS

The PUNCHLIST worksheet categorizes major work areas and suggests some commonly overlooked items for your inspection. Since the building inspections dealt primarily with health and safety issues, it's up to you to determine quality with your contractor.

Walk through the remodeled space with the worksheet in hand and carefully check all the suggested items. Take your time. The Punchlist assumes that all major work is done. If that is not the case, your project is not complete and the contractor should not be paid. Distinguish those items that must be done prior to your accepting the work and moving into the space from items that are really minor repairs. You are responsible for creating an inclusive list.

After you've completed your own inspection, arrange to meet with your contractor to discuss the items on your list and point out any areas of concern. When the contractor tells you how he will handle a particular item, mark it down on your Punchlist. When you're done filling in the Punchlist sheet, both you and your contractor should sign it. Keep a copy and give your contractor a copy as well so he can schedule the work in an orderly manner.

Your contractor needs to provide you with his notarized lien waiver along with those for each subcontractor. This is your proof that everyone has been paid for their materials and labor. When these items are in your possession and the agreed upon Punchlist items are complete, go ahead and issue final payment to your contractor. Keep the 10% retainage if there are any remaining items to be completed. It is the contractor's responsibility to complete them within 30 days. At that time you can release the retained payment.

CHECK IT:

CHECKLIST FOR PROJECT COMPLETION

❏ Make sure all major work is done prior to completing a final walk-through.

❏ Find a quiet time to do a Punchlist inspection on your own.

❏ Meet with your contractor to discuss the items on your list.

❏ Distinguish items that must be done prior to your accepting the work from items that are minor repairs.

❏ Get notarized lien waivers from your contractor for all who worked on your job.

❏ Issue final payment only after required Punchlist items are completed.

❏ Hold 10% retainage for 30 days to ensure minor items are completed.

As you enjoy your newly renovated home, think back through the entire process. You made it through all the planning, the mess, the strangers who joined you for morning coffee and all your worries and concerns. Congratulations on a job well done! Perhaps it's time to start thinking about your next home improvement project!

STEP 7

NOTES: PUNCHLIST ITEMS

_____

_____

_____

_____

_____

_____

_____

_____

_____

_____

_____

_____

_____

_____

_____

_____

_____

_____

_____

_____

_____

_____

_____

_____

_____

_____

PUNCHLIST

PAGE #1

Carpentry: all cabinets and counters installed and free from scratches and chips; baseboards complete with nail holes filled; all door knobs and cabinet hardware installed; interior doors trimmed for carpet clearance; closet shelves & poles installed and braced

1. _____
2. _____
3. _____
4. _____
5. _____
6. _____

Plumbing: fixtures caulked; dishwasher, ice maker, garbage disposal, hot water heater operational; toilet seats tight; bath accessories neatly mounted

1. _____
2. _____
3. _____
4. _____
5. _____
6. _____

STEP 7

PUNCHLIST
PAGE #2

Electric: all switches & outlets work properly; panel labeled; smoke detectors, electric appliances operational; cover plates straight and tight to wall

1. _____
2. _____
3. _____
4. _____
5. _____
6. _____

Heating: heat ducts vacuumed; vent hood, exhaust fans, furnace & thermostat operational; register covers installed

1. _____
2. _____
3. _____
4. _____
5. _____
6. _____

PUNCHLIST
PAGE #3

Drywall & Painting: doors painted on all sides & edges; spills and over-painting cleaned off windows, hinges, & floors; areas requiring touch-up

1. _____
2. _____
3. _____
4. _____
5. _____
6. _____

Miscellaneous: screens installed; cracked windows; interior areas cleaned up, other damage to be repaired

1. _____
2. _____
3. _____
4. _____
5. _____
6. _____

_____   _____
Owner   **Contractor**

_____
Date

STEP 7

PUNCHLIST
PAGE #4

Notes: areas of concern and contractor response.

_____

_____

_____

_____

_____

_____

_____

_____

_____

_____

_____

_____

_____

_____

_____

_____

_____

STEP 7

Appendices

Construction Standards

ITEM	POSSIBLE DEFECT	STANDARDS
Excavating & backfill	Ground settling around foundation, trenches, or other filled areas	Ground settling is normal but should not interfere with drainage away from the house. Contractor should fill the settled areas once. The homeowner is responsible for maintaining the grade once the contractor is finished.
Concrete & block	Basement or foundation wall cracks	Shrinkage cracks are normal unless they are in excess of 1/8". If such cracks exist, the contractor should repair them.
	Basement floor cracks	Hairline cracks in concrete floors are normal when under 3/16" in width. These cracks can be repaired by surface patching.
	Attached garage floor	Cracks over 1/4" wide are considered excessive. These cracks can be repair-ed by surface patching.
	Uneven concrete floors in basement	A concrete basement floor should not be so uneven that it cannot be used. It needs to meet standard tolerances.

ITEM	POSSIBLE DEFECT	STANDARDS
Concrete & block (cont'd)	Cracks in concrete slab on grade floors	Cracks which impair the performance of finish flooring are not acceptable. Cracks need to be filled so they are not apparent when the finish flooring is installed.
	Cracking, settling, or separating of concrete steps or stoops	Steps or stoops should not settle or separate beyond 1" from the house structure. Corrective measures are required to meet approved standards.
	Basement floor or walls wet	Dampness of basement walls or floors are common in new construction until the landscaping takes hold. Leaks can be caused by improper landscaping or failure to establish or maintain necessary site grading to ensure proper drainage.
Rough carpentry	Floors squeak	There is no guarantee for a squeak-proof floor, but fortunately "squeakiness" is often a temporary condition in new construction.
	Uneven wood floors	Floors should not be more than 1/4" out of level within a 9' square.
	Walls out of plumb	Walls should not be more than 1/2" out of plumb for any 8' vertical measure.
Roofing	Roof leaks	What appears to be a roof leak may actually be a leak around the flashing, especially at roof edges and penetrations like chimneys, skylights, and vents. Check to ensure flashing is tight. Roofs

ITEM	POSSIBLE DEFECT	STANDARDS
Roofing (cont'd)		should not leak under normal conditions except when there is ice build-up, high winds, or driving rain. Ice and snow build-ups are homeowner maintenance concerns. Water should drain from a flat roof, except for minor puddling.
	Leaks due to snow or rain coming into the attic through louvers or vents.	Attic and soffit vents are necessary to properly ventilate a house. Snow or rain will infiltrate depending on the force and direction of the wind.
Siding	Hardboard siding buckles & cracks	Hardboard siding is made from wood fibers bonded together with glue. Moisture makes it swell, crack, buckle and bend. Sealing this siding or painting it on all sides and edges helps prevent moisture infiltration.
	Delamination & joint separation	Siding should be installed according to manufacturer's standards. Delamination and joint separation are not acceptable and need corrective measures or replacement.
Gutters	Gutters & downspouts leak	Gutters and downspouts should not leak but will overflow in heavy rain. It is the homeowner's responsibility to keep gutters and downspouts free of debris and leaves.
Sealants	Leaks from exterior wall opening	Cracks and joints in exterior walls and around windows and doors should be properly caulked. It is

ITEM	POSSIBLE DEFECT	STANDARDS
Sealants (cont'd)		the contractor's responsibility to correct or repair caulk joints once during the first year warranty. Because caulk shrinks, it needs to be maintained periodically by the homeowner.
Exterior doors	Warping of wood or plastic doors	Exterior doors will warp slightly due to temperature differences between the interior and exterior surfaces. They should not, however, warp beyond 1/4" or to the degree they become inoperable. It is the contractor's responsibility to repair exterior doors once during the first year warranty.
Insulation	Insufficient insulation	Insulation should be installed according to applicable energy and building code requirements. Recommended R-values for insulation are determined by various climate zones. However, in most cases attics should have insulation equal to an R-38 value. Floors over unheated crawl spaces or basements in most homes should have an R-19 value. Exterior walls need at least an R-11 value while walls over crawl spaces will benefit from a value of R-19.
Drywall	Defects such as "nail pops", seam lines, cracked corners, trowel marks, bubbles, lack of smooth finish, blisters in tape, or other blemishes.	Slight imperfections such as "nail pops", seam lines and cracks are common in drywall installation. They are often caused by the house or addition settling and drying out after construction. However, more obvious defects

ITEM	POSSIBLE DEFECT	STANDARDS
Drywall (cont'd)		caused by poor workmanship (e.g., excessive compound in joints, trowel marks, cracked corners) are not acceptable. The contractor is responsible for correcting such defects to acceptable tolerance and repainting any repaired areas as necessary. The contractor is not, however, responsible for any color variations that result in the painting.
Ceramic tile	Ceramic tile cracks or loosens	Ceramic tile should not crack or loosen. The contractor is responsible for replacing any cracked tiles and re-securing loose tiles unless the problem was caused by the homeowner's negligence. The contractor is not responsible for discontinued patterns or color variations.
	Cracks in grout joints or where tile meets other materials, such as bathtubs	Cracks in the grouting are commonly caused by shrinkage, which is a normal condition. Regrouting cracks falls in the category of homeowner maintenance.
Vinyl flooring	"Nail pops" appear on surface	"Nail pops" showing through the surface of the flooring are not acceptable and need to be repaired. The contractor is responsible for correcting this condition by repairing or replacing flooring in the areas affected. Contractor is not responsible for discontinued patterns or color variations.

ITEM	POSSIBLE DEFECT	STANDARDS
Vinyl flooring (cont'd)	Flooring comes unglued	Vinyl flooring should not lift, bubble, or become unglued. The contractor is responsible for repairing the affected area but is not responsible for problems due to homeowner neglect.
	Seams or shrinkage gaps show	Seam gaps should not exceed 1/16". Where vinyl abuts to a different material, gaps should not exceed 1/8".
Hardwood flooring	Cracks develop between floor boards	Cracks should not exceed 1/16". The contractor is responsible for repairing these cracks within first year.
Carpeting	Seams show	Carpet seams will show, though there should be no visible gaps.
	Carpeting becomes loose, excessive stretching occurs, seams separate	When properly installed, wall-to-wall carpeting should not come up, become loose or separate where it's attached. The contractor is responsible for re-stretching and re-securing carpeting.
	Carpeting fades	Exposure to sunlight may cause spots or fading. Check with the manufacturer's warranty for liability and remedies.
Painting	Exterior paint or stain peels or fades	Fading of paint is normal over time, depending on natural climate conditions. There should not, however, be any fading or peeling during the first year. The contractor is responsible for preparing and refinishing affected areas and matching the color as closely as possible. If the deterio-

APPENDICES

ITEM	POSSIBLE DEFECT	STANDARDS
Painting (cont'd)		ration affects the majority of a wall, the whole wall should be refinished. Having newly painted areas does not extend the initial warranty period.
	Painting needs repair as a result of other repair work	Any repairs necessary to painting due to repair of other work is the contractor's responsibility. Necessary repairs should match surrounding areas as closely as possible.
	Varnish or lacquered finishes deteriorate	Varnish used on the exterior of a house will deteriorate rapidly. This deterioration is not the contractor's responsibility. Varnish and lacquer on interior finishes should not deteriorate in the first year. Interior areas should be touched up, matching the color as closely as possible.
	Interior painting coverage spotty, does not visually cover walls or trim	Primer should always be used because it creates a strong bond between wall and paint, helps fill in cracks, resists moisture, and seals the surface so finish coats are smoother and more uniform. Inside, primer should be used on all bare wood, new drywall, patched areas, new trim, and areas stained by water marks, crayons, or ink. Exterior areas for primer include bare wood and patched areas. Paint should be applied so it visually covers all areas.
	Mildew & fungus on painted surfaces	Mildew and fungus form on painted surfaces exposed to unusual moisture. Moisture can

ITEM	POSSIBLE DEFECT	STANDARDS
Painting (cont'd)		be due to proximity to a body of water, excessive rainfall, or humidity. This is a homeowner maintenance issue.
Fireplace	Does not draw properly	High winds can cause temporary negative draft situations. The problem might also be caused by large branches or trees too close to the chimney. Determine whether the malfunction is caused by design, construction, or natural conditions.
Heating	Dampers & registers out of balance	The homeowner is responsible for balancing dampers and registers.
	Noisy ductwork	As metal heats and cools, it contracts and expands. This results in sounds that are generally acceptable. The ductwork should not, however, "oilcan" and cause a booming sound. The contractor is responsible for eliminating "oil-canning". It is most often caused when the wrong gauge of metal is used for the ductwork.
Plumbing	Leaking faucet & valves	Unless there are defects in workmanship or materials, new faucets and valves should not leak. Leakage at a later point can be caused by worn washers, and replacement is part of homeowner's maintenance.
	Defective plumbing fixtures, appliances, or trim	All new fixtures, fittings, and appliances should conform with their manufacturers' standards. If the contractor supplied the materials, he is responsible for replac-

ITEM	POSSIBLE DEFECT	STANDARDS
Plumbing (cont'd)		ing any fixture or fitting that does not meet standards.
	Chips or cracks on fixture surfaces	Chips and cracks on tubs, shower units, and sinks can occur when the surface is hit with a sharp or heavy object. The contractor is to repair any cracks or chips noted before construction was complete.
	Noisy water pipes)	Noise can be caused by water flow and pipe expansion and is considered within standard tolerances. Pipe vibrations or loud "water hammer" noises are the contractor's responsibility to correct.
	Plumbing lines freeze and burst	Plumbing lines should be adequately protected during anticipated cold weather. If caused by the contractor's negligence and lack of protection, the contractor is responsible for correcting the condition that caused the freezing and for repairing the damage. If damage was the result of homeowner neglect, the contractor is not responsible.
Electric	Fuses blow, circuit breaker kicks off	Fuses and circuit breakers should not kick or blow under normal usage. Wiring should be checked for conformity with code requirements. Contractor is responsible for all new wiring installed that does not meet code regulations.
	Switches & outlets are not all operational	All switches and outlets should function as intended. If outlet

ITEM	POSSIBLE DEFECT	STANDARDS
Electric (cont'd)		appears not to be working, it maybe a "switched outlet" (connected to a wall switch) and should work when the wall switch is turned on. Contractor is responsible for repair or replacement of defective switches and outlets.
	Ground fault interrupter trips frequently	Ground fault interrupters (gfi) are designed as safety devices to protect against electrical shock. GFI requirements are determined by electrical code. Tripping can happen easily and, unless due to a material or construction defect, is to be expected.
	Drafts from electrical outlets	This is normal in new construction wherever electrical junction boxes in exterior walls produce an air flow and cold air is drawn through the outlets.

Contract Documents

This sample contract is provided as a service. Consider it carefully and discuss it with your attorney. No standard form can meet all requirements. It is believed to be reliable but is not guaranteed.

BUILDING & REMODELING CONTRACT

Contract made this _____ day of _____ , ___ (year), between _____

hereinafter referred to as OWNER residing at _____ and

_____ , hereinafter

referred to as CONTRACTOR, with offices at _____

The parties to this Agreement, in consideration of the mutual covenants and stipulations set out, agree to the Scope of Work as set forth in the Contract plans and specifications, all written addenda mutually agreed upon and issued prior to the execution of this Agreement, and all written modifications mutually issued by the Owner and Contractor after execution of the Contract including Change Orders. These form the Contract Documents and are fully part of the Contract.

SECTION I

CONTRACT AS ENTIRE AGREEMENT

This Contract contains the entire agreement between the parties, and no statements, promises, or inducements made by either party or agent of either party that are not contained in this contract shall be valid or binding; this Contract may not be enlarged, modified or altered except in writing signed by both parties and endorsed on this Agreement.

SECTION II

AGREEMENT

ARTICLE 1. SCOPE OF THE WORK

The Contractor shall furnish all of the materials and perform all of the Work as described in the Contract Documents as it pertains to the work to be performed on the property at:

ARTICLE 2. TIME OF COMPLETION

2.1   The work to be performed under this Contract shall be commenced on or before, _____ and shall be substantially completed on or before _____ .

2.2   Owner will furnish to Contractor, prior to commencement of the Work, reasonable evidence of financial ability to fulfill the Owner's obligation under this Contract.

2.3   Contractor agrees to start and diligently pursue the Work through completion. However, Substantial Completion may be extended because of delays beyond the Contractor's control, including but not limited to: Delays in issuance of necessary building permits, adverse weather conditions, availability of materials or labor, illness, unavoidable casualties, any act or neglect of Owner, architect or designer, additional work or changes requested by Owner, failure of Owner to make payments when due, delays occasioned by acts of God, strikes, changes in governmental regulations, catastrophes, wars, riots and all similar occurrences beyond Contractor's, his subcontractors' or suppliers' control.

2.4   Owner agrees that the date of Substantial Completion may be extended for a reasonable period of time without incurring damages or penalty for such delays.

2.5   Substantial Completion is that date when the Work is sufficiently completed as to obtain any final inspections stipulated by the building permit or when the OWNER can occupy, utilize or continue the Work in conjunction with the use for which it was intended, whichever occurs first.

ARTICLE 3. THE CONTRACT PRICE

3.1   The Owner shall pay the Contractor for the performance of the Work under the Contract the sum of _____ Dollars ($ _____), subject to additions and deductions pursuant to authorized Change Orders.

3.2   Upon reasonable request by Owner, the Contractor will make alterations, additions or substitutions to the Work and Contract price, and Substantial Completion will be modified accordingly, as set out in a written Change Order. All Change Orders shall be in writing and signed by both Owner and Contractor, and shall be incorporated in and become part of the Contract.

3.3   Any adjustment in the Contract price resulting in a credit or a charge to the Owner will be determined by mutual consent of the parties, before starting the work involved in the change. In some cases a deposit will be required before starting the work and, in all cases, changes will be paid in full upon completion of the change order work.

3.4   Owner agrees to make requests concerning any changes, additions or substitutions directly to the Contractor and not to his workers or subcontractors on the worksite.

3.5   If the Contract price and specifications include allowances, and the cost is greater or less than the allowance figure included, the Contract price will be adjusted accordingly.

ARTICLE 4.   PROGRESS PAYMENTS

4.1   Based upon applications for payment submitted to the Owner by the Contractor, the Owner shall make progress payments on account of the Contract Sum to the Contractor as follows: All payments shall be due on the day indicated.

_____

_____

_____

_____

_____

_____

_____

4.2   Any monies not paid in accordance with the Contract Documents shall bear interest from the date payment is due at 1% per month.

4.3   Payments may be withheld without interest, from Contractor by Owner, in an amount equal to the Work in question, due to significantly defective Work not remedied or persistent failure by Contractor to carry out the work in accordance with the Contract Documents.

4.4   Final payment, constituting the entire unpaid balance of the Contract Sum, shall be paid by the Owner to the Contractor no more than 30 days after the Work is entirely complete.

4.5   The Contractor will furnish the Owner appropriate releases or lien waivers for all work performed or materials provided at the time the next periodic payment shall be due. Final payment will not be due until Contractor delivers to Owner a complete release of all liens arising out of this agreement. If any lien remains unsatisfied after all payments are made, Contractor will refund to Owner all monies paid by Owner to discharge such lien, including all cost and reasonable attorney's fees.

ARTICLE 5. GENERAL PROVISIONS

5.1   All work shall be completed in a workman-like manner and in compliance with all building codes and other applicable laws.

5.2   To the extent required by law all work shall be performed by individuals duly licensed and authorized by law to perform said work.

5.3   The Contractor may at his discretion engage subcontractors to perform work hereunder, provided the Contractor shall fully pay said subcontractors and in all instances remain responsible for the proper completion of this contract.

5.4   The Owner will have no authority to negotiate with Contractor's workers or subcontractors or to directly subcontract any of the Work described herein or to have any subcontractor work at the site under the terms of this Contract without the written approval of the Contractor.

5.5   The Contractor will have sole control of the construction personnel, including subcontractors. Owner will not issue any instructions or otherwise interfere with construction personnel, including subcontractors.

5.6   The Contractor warrants he is adequately insured for injury to his employees and others incurring loss or injury as a result of the acts of the Contractor or his employees or subcontractors. Certificates of general liability and workman's compensation will be sent to Owner prior to any work beginning.

5.7   The Contractor agrees to remove all debris and leave the premises in broom clean condition.

5.8   In the event the Owner shall fail to pay any periodic or installment payment due hereunder, the Contractor may cease work without breach, pending payment or resolution of any dispute.

5.9   The Contractor warrants all work for a period of _____ months following completion.

5.10   All disputes hereunder shall be resolved by binding arbitration in accordance with the American Arbitration Association. Notwithstanding this provision, nothing will preclude Contractor's right to pursue the lien remedies and procedures as provided within the laws of _____ (your state).

5.11   If either party becomes involved in arbitration or litigation arising out of this agreement or its performance, reasonable cost and expense of arbitration and attorney's fees may be awarded to the party who recovers judgment.

5.12   Other provisions:

_____

_____

_____

_____

_____

_____

ARTICLE 6. TERMINATION AND DEFAULT.

6.1   If Owner fails to comply with the provisions of this Contract, Contractor may terminate this Contract and retain any deposit or Monies received as liquidated damages, or at the option of the Contractor, Contractor may proceed for specific performance or any other available legal or equitable remedies.

Owner will be in default under this Contract if any of the following take place:
    a.   Owner fails or refuses to pay within five (5) days any amount set forth in this Agreement.
    b.   Owner in any way fails or refuses to perform any provision of this Agreement required of Owner.
    c.   Owner makes any assignment for benefit of creditors or files any petition under any bankruptcy, insolvency or debtor relief law.

6.2   If Contractor fails to comply with the provisions of this Contract, Owner may terminate this Contract.
Contractor will be in default under this Contract if any of the following take place:
    a.   Contractor fails or refuses to do the Work in accordance with the Contract Documents after ten (10) days written notice from Owner.
    b.   Contractor makes any assignment for benefit of creditors or files any petition under any bankruptcy, insolvency or debtor relief law.

SECTION III

EFFECT OF AGREEMENT

This agreement shall inure to the benefit of and be binding on the heirs, executors, assignees and successors of the respective parties. Neither party will have the right to assign, transfer or sublet his/her interests or obligations hereunder without the written consent of the other party. If two or more parties are named herein as OWNER, their obligation will be joint and several.

IN WITNESS WHEREOF, the parties have executed this agreement on the day and year first above written.

_____	_____
OWNER'S NAME	CONTRACTOR'S NAME
_____	_____
OWNER'S SIGNATURE	CONTRACTOR'S SIGNATURE

CHANGE ORDER AUTHORIZATION

Change Order # _____

Property Address: _____

Date: _____

Description of additional work or changes: Cost:

_____   _____

_____   _____

_____   _____

_____   _____

_____   _____

_____   _____

Original Contract Price . . . .$ _____

Net Change by previous Change Orders . . . .$ _____

Current Change Order # _____ . . . .$ _____

Amended Contract Price . . . .$ _____

The Contract Time will be increased/decreased/unchanged by _____ (   ) days

_____   _____
Homeowner   Contractor

_____   _____
Dated   Dated

WAIVER OF LIEN

KNOW ALL MEN BY THESE PRESENT: That I, the undersigned contractor or subcontractor, having furnished labor and/or materials for construction at _____ _____ (the premises), for and in consideration of _____ Dollars ($ _____) and other good and valuable consideration, to me paid, the receipt whereof is hereby acknowledged, do hereby waive, release, and relinquish any and all rights to file liens against said premises for materials and/or services or labor provided to this date. This discharge of lien will not constitute a release or discharge of any claim for moniesnow, or hereinfter, due for said services and/or materials, if existing.

This release is binding upon and inures to the benefit of the parties, their successors, and designated representatives.

Dated this_____day of _____ , _____ (year).

By: _____

Contractor/Subcontractor

_____

Address

_____

State of}

County of}

On this _____ day of _____ , 199__, before me, appeared _____ personally known to me (or proved to me on the basis of satisfactory evidence) to be the person(s) whose name(s) is/are subscribed to the within instrument and acknowledged to me that he/she/they executed the same in his/her/their authorized capacity(ies), and that by his/her/their signature(s) on the instrument the person(s), or the entity upon behalf of which the person(s) acted, executed the instrument.

WITNESS my hand and official seal

_____

Signature of Notary   (Seal)

Appendix C

Worksheets

WISHLIST WORKSHEET

Room: _____   **Room Size:** _____

Design ideas I'd love to include:

_____   _____

_____   _____

_____   _____

_____   _____

_____   _____

_____   _____

_____   _____

_____   _____

Specific products I want to include: (Refer to your notebook and list products wherever possible.)

_____   _____

_____   _____

_____   _____

_____   _____

_____   _____

SKETCH OF EXISTING LAYOUT WORKSHEET

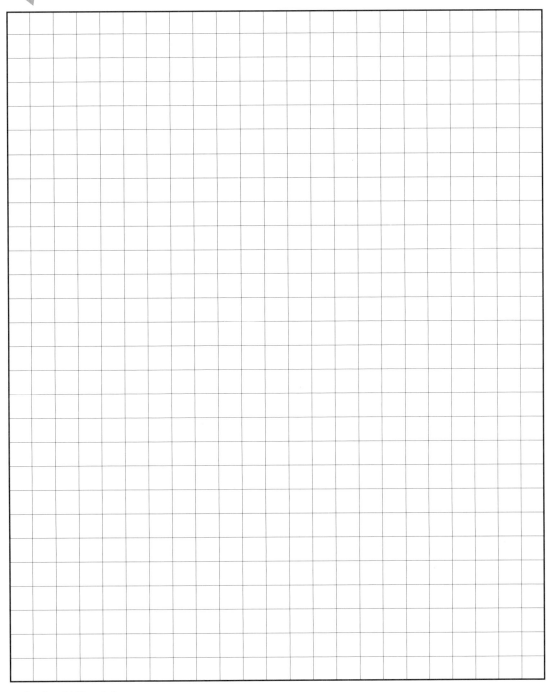

Scale 1/4″ = 1 ft

SKETCH OF NEW PLAN WORKSHEET

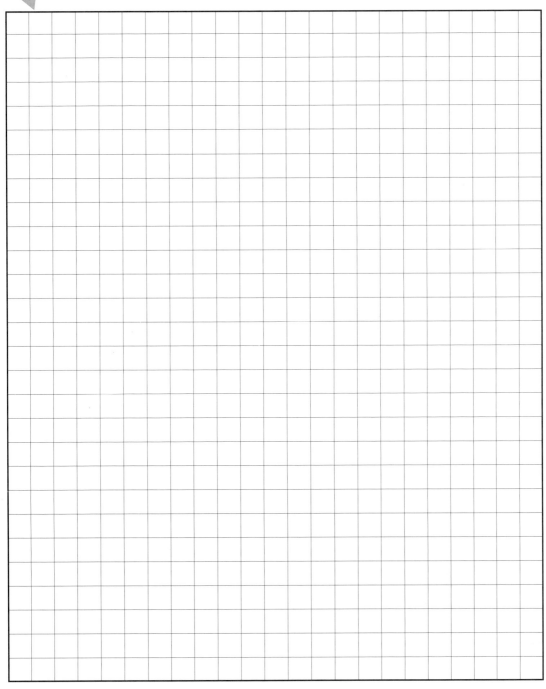

Scale 1/4" = 1 ft

Financial Worksheet

MONTHLY INCOME

Gross Monthly Income _____

Commissions _____

Bonuses _____

Dividend/Interest Income _____

Business/Investment Income _____

Pensions/Social Security _____

Alimony/Child Support _____

Rental Income _____

TOTAL MONTHLY INCOME $ _____

MONTHLY EXPENSES

	Current Balance Owed	Monthly Payment
Car Payment	_____	_____
Student Loans	_____	_____
Medical Payments	_____	_____
Credit Cards:		
name _____		
acct # _____	_____	_____
name _____		
acct # _____	_____	_____
name _____		
acct # _____	_____	_____
name _____		
acct # _____	_____	_____

	Current Balance Owed	Monthly Payment
name _____	_____	_____
acct# _____	_____	_____
Alimony/Child Support	_____	_____
Other	_____	_____
Other	_____	_____

TOTAL MONTHLY INCOME $ _____

		Cash or Market Value
SAVINGS/ASSETS:		
Bank Accounts		
name _____	acct # _____	_____
name _____	acct # _____	_____
name _____	acct # _____	_____
Brokerage Accounts		
name _____	acct# _____	_____
name _____	acct # _____	_____
Stocks & Bonds		_____
Life Insurance Cash Value		_____
Real Estate Owned		_____
Other		_____

PRELIMINARY COSTS WORKSHEET

WISHLIST ITEM	PROJECTED COST
1. _____	_____
2. _____	_____
3. _____	_____
4. _____	_____
5. _____	_____
6. _____	_____
7. _____	_____
8. _____	_____
9. _____	_____
10. _____	_____
11. _____	_____
12. _____	_____
13. _____	_____
14. _____	_____
15. _____	_____
16. _____	_____
17. _____	_____
18. _____	_____
19. _____	_____
20. _____	_____

WISHLIST ITEM	PROJECTED COST
21. _____	_____
22. _____	_____
23. _____	_____
24. _____	_____
25. _____	_____
26. _____	_____
27. _____	_____
28. _____	_____
29. _____	_____
30. _____	_____

Subtotal $ _____

Contingencies @15% $ _____

Professional Fees @ 5% $ _____

TOTAL $ _____

PROJECT PRIORITIES WORKSHEET

MUST HAVE	NICE TO HAVE
1. _____	16. _____
2. _____	17. _____
3. _____	18. _____
4. _____	19. _____
5. _____	20. _____
6. _____	21. _____
7. _____	22. _____
8. _____	23. _____
9. _____	24. _____
10._____	25. _____
11._____	26. _____
12._____	27. _____
13._____	28. _____
14._____	29. _____
15._____	30. _____

Consider this list your master plan as you approach your project. By distinguishing your needs from your wants, you can stage your remodeling and work within your budget.

PROJECT DRAWING WORKSHEET

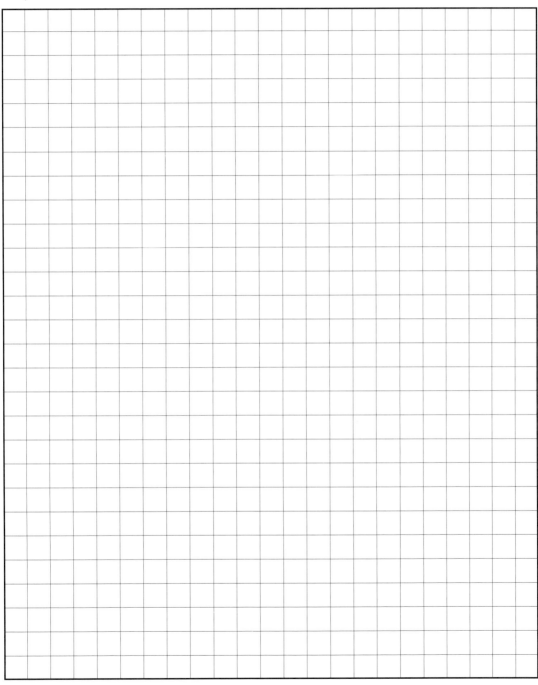

Scale 1/4″ = 1 ft

DESIGNERS REFERENCES WORKSHEET

Client: _____

Phone: _____

Type of project: _____

Client: _____

Phone: _____

Type of project: _____

Client: _____

Phone: _____

Type of project: _____

QUESTIONS TO ASK:

1. Was (s)he creative and good at problem solving?

_____

_____

_____

2. Did (s)he keep your goals and concerns in mind?

_____

_____

_____

3. Was (s)he easy to work with?

_____

_____

_____

4. Were your drawings complete and satisfactory to your contractor?

_____

_____

_____

5. Were there any problems that specifically arose from the design?

_____

_____

_____

6. Were his/her initial price estimates accurate? Did your project come in on budget?

_____

_____

_____

7. Did (s)he meet deadlines?

_____

_____

_____

8. Was there anything about your project that could have been done better?

_____

_____

_____

◄SPECIFICATIONS WORKSHEET————————

WORKPLAN

1. _____
2. _____
3. _____
4. _____
5. _____
6. _____
7. _____
8. _____
9. _____
10. _____
11. _____
12. _____
13. _____
14. _____
15. _____
16. _____
17. _____
18. _____
19. _____
20. _____

DETAILS

1. _____
2. _____
3. _____
4. _____
5. _____
6. _____
7. _____
8. _____
9. _____
10. _____
11. _____
12. _____
13. _____
14. _____
15. _____
16. _____
17. _____
18. _____
19. _____
20. _____

WORKPLAN	DETAILS
21. _____	21. _____
22. _____	22. _____
23. _____	23. _____
24. _____	24. _____
25. _____	25. _____
26. _____	26. _____
27. _____	27. _____
28. _____	28. _____
29. _____	29. _____
30. _____	30. _____

Miscellaneous: _____

_____

_____

_____

_____

_____

_____

_____

_____

_____

Bid Sheet Worksheet

Contractor: _____

Phone #: _____

1. Demolition & Debris Removal $ _____
2. Excavation _____
3. Concrete & Masonry _____
4. Framing _____
5. Lumber _____
6. Windows & Doors _____
7. Siding _____
8. Roofing _____
9. Gutters _____
10. Landscaping _____
11. Insulation _____
12. Plumbing _____
13. Heating _____
14. Electric _____
15. Drywall _____
16. Finish Carpentry _____
17. Painting _____
18. Cabinets & Counter Tops _____
19. Plumbing Fixtures _____
20. Lighting Fixtures _____
21. Flooring _____
22. Ceramic Tile _____
23. Hardware _____
24. Miscellaneous Conditions _____
25. Specialty Items _____

TOTAL BID $ _____

Contractor Interview Worksheet ────────────

NAME _____

COMPANY NAME _____   Phone: _____

ADDRESS: _____   Mobile: _____

_____   Fax: _____

Questions to ask at your first meeting:

1. How long have you been in business? _____

2. Are you licensed? _____ For how long? _____ License # _____

3. What insurance do you carry? _____

4. What types of projects are you currently doing? _____

5. How many jobs are you doing right now? _____

6. How does my job fit into your schedule? _____

7. Who will be supervising my job? _____

8. What warranties do you provide? _____

9. How do you handle changes once the job begins? _____

After receiving bids:

1. Please provide 5 CUSTOMER REFERENCES.

Name: _____   Phone: _____

Name: _____   Phone: _____

Name: _____   Phone: _____

Name: _____   Phone: _____

Name: _____   Phone: _____

2. May I have 3 TRADE/CREDIT references?

Name: _____ Phone: _____

Name: _____ Phone: _____

Name: _____ Phone: _____

3. May I visit one of your job sites? _____

4. When could you start? _____

5. How much time will it take to complete my project? _____

6. Can you provide me with a sample contract? _____

CONTRACTOR'S REFERENCES WORKSHEET

Contractor Name: _____

Customer Name: _____ Phone: _____

Project Description: _____

1. Was it easy to work with this contractor? _____

2. Were you happy with the quality of the work? _____

3. Was your job done on schedule? _____

4. Was (s)he responsive to your concerns? _____

5. Did (s)he perform a daily clean-up? _____

6. Was the job kept orderly and neat? _____

7. Was the contractor good at problem solving? _____

8. Were you pleased with his/her subcontractors' work? _____

9. Did this contractor supply daily on-site supervision? _____

10. Were there many change orders? _____

11. Did the contractor return to complete final details? _____

12. Would you use him/her again? _____

13. What did you like about him/her? _____

14. Did you have particular dislikes about him/her? _____

_____

_____

_____

_____

_____

Individual Bid Review Worksheet

Contractor #1: _____ **Start date:** _____

Project duration: _____

WORKPLAN ITEM & DETAIL	INCLUDED IN BID

1. _____ YES ____ NO _____

2. _____ YES ____ NO _____

3. _____ YES ____ NO _____

4. _____ YES ____ NO _____

5. _____ YES ____ NO _____

6. _____ YES ____ NO _____

7. _____ YES ____ NO _____

8. _____ YES ____ NO _____

9. _____ YES ____ NO _____

10. _____ YES ____ NO _____

11. _____ YES ____ NO _____

12. _____ YES ____ NO _____

13. _____ YES ____ NO _____

14. _____ YES ____ NO _____

15. _____ YES ____ NO _____

16. _____ YES ____ NO _____

17. _____ YES ____ NO _____

WORKPLAN ITEM & DETAIL	INCLUDED IN BID

18. _____ YES ____ NO _____

19. _____ YES ____ NO _____

20. _____ YES ____ NO _____

21. _____ YES ____ NO _____

22. _____ YES ____ NO _____

23. _____ YES ____ NO _____

24. _____ YES ____ NO _____

25. _____ YES ____ NO _____

Questions about this bid:

_____

_____

_____

_____

_____

_____

_____

_____

Individual Bid Review Worksheet

Contractor #2: _____ **Start date:** _____

Project duration: _____

WORKPLAN ITEM & DETAIL	INCLUDED IN BID

1. _____ YES ____ NO _____

2. _____ YES ____ NO _____

3. _____ YES ____ NO _____

4. _____ YES ____ NO _____

5. _____ YES ____ NO _____

6. _____ YES ____ NO _____

7. _____ YES ____ NO _____

8. _____ YES ____ NO _____

9. _____ YES ____ NO _____

10. _____ YES ____ NO _____

11. _____ YES ____ NO _____

12. _____ YES ____ NO _____

13. _____ YES ____ NO _____

14. _____ YES ____ NO _____

15. _____ YES ____ NO _____

16. _____ YES ____ NO _____

17. _____ YES ____ NO _____

WORKPLAN ITEM & DETAIL   **INCLUDED IN BID**

18. _____ YES ____ NO _____

19. _____ YES ____ NO _____

20. _____ YES ____ NO _____

21. _____ YES ____ NO _____

22. _____ YES ____ NO _____

23. _____ YES ____ NO _____

24. _____ YES ____ NO _____

25. _____ YES ____ NO _____

Questions about this bid:

_____

_____

_____

_____

_____

_____

_____

_____

INDIVIDUAL BID REVIEW WORKSHEET

Contractor #3: _____ Start date: _____

Project duration: _____

WORKPLAN ITEM & DETAIL   INCLUDED IN BID

1. _____ YES ____ NO _____
2. _____ YES ____ NO _____
3. _____ YES ____ NO _____
4. _____ YES ____ NO _____
5. _____ YES ____ NO _____
6. _____ YES ____ NO _____
7. _____ YES ____ NO _____
8. _____ YES ____ NO _____
9. _____ YES ____ NO _____
10. _____ YES ____ NO _____
11. _____ YES ____ NO _____
12. _____ YES ____ NO _____
13. _____ YES ____ NO _____
14. _____ YES ____ NO _____
15. _____ YES ____ NO _____
16. _____ YES ____ NO _____
17. _____ YES ____ NO _____

WORKPLAN ITEM & DETAIL		**INCLUDED IN BID**	

18. _____ YES ____ NO _____

19. _____ YES ____ NO _____

20. _____ YES ____ NO _____

21. _____ YES ____ NO _____

22. _____ YES ____ NO _____

23. _____ YES ____ NO _____

24. _____ YES ____ NO _____

25. _____ YES ____ NO _____

QUESTIONS ABOUT THIS BID:

_____

_____

_____

_____

_____

_____

_____

_____

BID COMPARISON WORKSHEET

	BID #1	BID #2	BID #3
1. Demolition/Debris Removal	_____	_____	_____
2. Excavation	_____	_____	_____
3. Concrete & Masonry	_____	_____	_____
4. Framing	_____	_____	_____
5. Lumber	_____	_____	_____
6. Windows & Doors	_____	_____	_____
7. Siding	_____	_____	_____
8. Roofing	_____	_____	_____
9. Gutters	_____	_____	_____
10. Landscaping	_____	_____	_____
11. Insulation	_____	_____	_____
12. Plumbing	_____	_____	_____
13. Heating	_____	_____	_____
14. Electric	_____	_____	_____
15. Drywall	_____	_____	_____
16. Finish Carpentry	_____	_____	_____
17. Painting	_____	_____	_____
18. Cabinets & Counter Tops	_____	_____	_____
19. Plumbing Fixtures	_____	_____	_____
20. Lighting Fixtures	_____	_____	_____

	BID #1	BID #2	BID #3
21. Flooring			
22. Ceramic Tile			
23. Hardware			
24. Miscellaneous Conditions			
25. Specialty Items			
TOTAL BID $			

Contract Information Worksheet

CONTRACTOR _____

COMPANY NAME _____

ADDRESS (not PO Box) _____

PHONE: _____ PAGER: _____ FAX: _____

LICENSE # (if applicable) _____

OVERALL SCOPE OF PROJECT:

_____

_____

OTHER ITEMS TO BE DONE: Include surveys, zoning and/or building permits

   BY OWNER:

_____

_____

   BY CONTRACTOR:

_____

_____

   BY ARCHITECT/ENGINEER/DESIGNER

_____

_____

START DATE _____ EST. COMPLETION DATE _____

TOTAL CONTRACT PRICE _____

PAYMENT SCHEDULE:

WORK COMPLETED   PAYMENT AMOUNT

_____   _____

_____   _____

_____   _____

_____   _____

_____   _____

_____   _____

LIST OF ADDENDUM TO ATTACH:

_____

_____

_____

_____

_____

_____

RECEIVED: YES   NO

INSURANCE CERTIFICATES   ☐   ☐

LIST OF SUBCONTRACTORS   ☐   ☐

Carpentry: all cabinets and counters installed and free from scratches and chips; baseboards complete with nail holes filled; all door knobs and cabinet hardware installed; interior doors trimmed for carpet clearance; closet shelves & poles installed and braced

1. _____
2. _____
3. _____
4. _____
5. _____
6. _____

Plumbing: fixtures caulked; dishwasher, ice maker, garbage disposal, hot water heater operational; toilet seats tight; bath accessories neatly mounted

1. _____
2. _____
3. _____
4. _____
5. _____
6. _____

◀ PUNCHLIST ──────────────────────────────

PAGE #2

Electric: all switches & outlets work properly; panel labeled; smoke detectors, electric appliances operational; cover plates straight and tight to wall

1. _____
2. _____
3. _____
4. _____
5. _____
6. _____

Heating: heat ducts vacuumed; vent hood, exhaust fans, furnace & thermostat operational; register covers installed

1. _____
2. _____
3. _____
4. _____
5. _____
6. _____

Drywall & Painting: doors painted on all sides & edges; spills and over-painting cleaned off windows, hinges, & floors; areas requiring touch-up

1. _____
2. _____
3. _____
4. _____
5. _____
6. _____

Miscellaneous: screens installed; cracked windows; interior areas cleaned up, other damage to be repaired

1. _____
2. _____
3. _____
4. _____
5. _____
6. _____

_____   _____
Owner   **Contractor**

_____
Date

PUNCHLIST
PAGE #4

Notes: areas of concern and contractor response.

_____

_____

_____

_____

_____

_____

_____

_____

_____

_____

_____

_____

_____

_____

_____

_____

_____

NOTES:

NOTES:

_____

_____

_____

_____

_____

_____

_____

_____

_____

_____

_____

_____

_____

_____

_____

_____

_____

_____

_____

_____

_____

_____

_____

_____

_____

_____

_____

_____

APPENDICES

QUICK ORDER FORM

Fax Orders: (716) 244-0053. Send this form.

E-mail orders: orders@www.homesmart.org

Postal orders: HomeSmart Consulting
    PO Box 18306
    Rochester, New York 14618-8306

YES, please send Fearless Remodeling to the address below. Enclosed is a check or money order for $24.95. (Books are sent priority mail. $24.95 per copy plus $4.00 shipping and handling for the first book, $1.95 for each additional copy to the same address. Payable in U.S. funds. New York State residents, please add 8% sales tax.

Name_____

Street Address_____

City_____ State_____ Zip Code_____

Payment: ___check ___credit card: ___Visa, ___MasterCard

Card number: _____

Name on Card: _____ Exp. date: _____/_____

QUICK ORDER FORM

Fax Orders: (716) 244-0053. Send this form.

E-mail orders: orders@www.homesmart.org

Postal orders: HomeSmart Consulting
PO Box 18306
Rochester, New York 14618-8306

YES, please send Fearless Remodeling to the address below. Enclosed is a
check or money order for $24.95. (Books are sent priority mail. $24.95 per
copy plus $4.00 shipping and handling for the first book, $1.95 for each
additional copy to the same address. Payable in U.S. funds. New York State
residents, please add 8% sales tax.

Name_____

Street Address_____

City_____ State_____ Zip Code_____

Payment: __check __credit card: __Visa, __MasterCard

Card number: _____

Name on Card: _____ Exp. date: _____ /_____